LASTING DIFFERENCES

HIGH/SCOPE
EDUCATIONAL RESEARCH FOUNDATION
Ypsilanti, Michigan

Monographs of the
High/Scope Educational Research Foundation
Number Twelve

LASTING DIFFERENCES

The High/Scope Preschool Curriculum Comparison Study Through Age 23

Lawrence J. Schweinhart
David P. Weikart

commentaries by

Rolf Loeber
University of Pittsburgh

George S. Morrison
University of North Texas

Kathy Sylva
University of London

Valora Washington
W. K. Kellogg Foundation

HIGH/SCOPE PRESS

Published by
High/Scope® Press

A Division of the
High/Scope Educational Research Foundation
600 North River Street
Ypsilanti, Michigan 48198-2898
(313)485-2000, FAX (313)485-0704

Marge Senninger, High/Scope Press Editor

Linda Eckel, Cover and Text Design

Library of Congress Cataloging-in-Publication Data

Schweinhart. L. J. (Lawrence J.) 1947–
Lasting Differences: the High/Scope Preschool Curriculum Comparison Study through age 23 / Lawrence J. Schweinhart, David P. Weikart; commentaries by Rolf Loeber. . . [et al.].
p. cm. — (Monographs of the High/Scope Educational Research Foundation ; no. 12)
Includes bibliographical references (p.) and index.
ISBN 1-57379-017-6
1. High/Scope Preschool Curriculum Comparison Study (Ypsilanti, Mich.) 2. Socially handicapped children—Education (Preschool)—Michigan—Ypsilanti—Curricula—Longitudinal studies. 3. Education, Preschool—Michigan—Ypsilanti—Curricula—Longitudinal studies. 4. School children —Michigan—Ypsilanti—Social conditions—Longitudinal studies. 5. Social adjustment—Michigan—Ypsilanti—Longitudinal studies. 6. Educational surveys—Michigan—Ypsilanti. I. Weikart, David P. II. Title. III. Series
LC 4092.M42S367 1997
371.96'7'0977435—dc20 96-43660
CIP

Printed in the United States of America

Contents

Tables and Figures

Tables

Figures

Acknowledgments

The authors gratefully acknowledge the contributions of Van Loggins, who went to some extraordinary lengths to find and interview study participants at age 23; Helen Barnes, who coordinated data collection, coding, and entry; Anthony North, who helped analyze the data; Mark Feldkamp, David Tholen, and David Mackoff-Borisy, who collected data from crime records; Nancy Burandt, who coded and entered the data; Marge Yahrmatter, who helped prepare the tables; Ann Epstein, who reviewed the report; Marge Senninger, who carefully edited the manuscript; and Diana Knepp, who typeset the tables and prepared the manuscript for typesetting. We thank the Ford Foundation and the U.S. Administration for Children and Families for funding the data collection and a donor (who wishes to remain anonymous) for funding the data analysis and report writing. Finally, we thank the study participants and their families, without whose cooperation this study could not have been conducted.

Executive Summary

The High/Scope Preschool Curriculum Comparison Study Through Age 23

Now with data through age 23, the High/Scope Preschool Curriculum Comparison Study assesses the relative effectiveness of three preschool curriculum models. At the outset of the study, 68 three- and four-year-old children who were living in poverty and at risk of school failure were each randomly assigned to one of three groups. Each group experienced a preschool program employing one of the following curriculum models:

- The **Direct Instruction** model, in which teachers initiated activities and children responded, adhering to a script with academic objectives for the children.
- A traditional **Nursery School** model, in which teachers responded to activities that children initiated, with a minimum of structure.
- The **High/Scope** model, in which teachers and children both initiated activities appropriate to children's developmental levels; teachers arranged the classroom and the daily routine so children could plan, do, and review their own activities and so teachers could support children as they engaged in key learning experiences.

Program staff implemented each curriculum model independently and to the highest standards, conducting 2½-hour classes 5 days a week and 1½-hour home visits biweekly, when the study children were 3 and 4 years old. Except for the use of different curriculum models, all aspects of program implementation were identical across the three curriculum groups.

After almost annual follow-ups of children in the three curriculum groups through age 10, the most important finding was that overall, the average IQ of the three groups had risen 27 points after the first year of their preschool program. However, except for the fact that the Direct Instruction group had an average IQ significantly higher than that of the Nursery School group at the end of the preschool program, the three groups differed little from one another on a variety of tests used in the various follow-ups through age 10. Thus, the conclusion at that point in the study was that well-implemented preschool curriculum models have similar effects on children's intellectual and academic performance.

At the age-15 follow-up, however, when the measurement of outcomes was expanded beyond intellectual and academic tests to include examining community behavior, the Direct Instruction group reported committing significantly more acts of misconduct than the High/Scope group — indeed, 2½ times as many. In addition, the Direct Instruction group had significantly fewer members appointed to a school job or office than did the Nursery School group, and significantly fewer members of the Direct

Instruction group than of the other groups were well thought of by their families or participated in sports.

Now, from the study's age-23 findings, the clear conclusion is that the High/Scope and Nursery School groups are better-off than the Direct Instruction group in a variety of ways. Either the High/Scope group or the Nursery School group, or both, show statistically significant advantages over the Direct Instruction group on 17 variables. Most important, compared with the Direct Instruction group, the High/Scope and Nursery School groups have had significantly fewer felony arrests of various kinds, fewer years of special education for emotional impairment, and more members doing volunteer work. In addition, compared with the Direct Instruction group, the High/Scope group has identified fewer people in the community who "gave them a hard time," aspires to achieving a higher level of schooling, and has more members living with their spouse, while the Nursery School group ranks lower in number of times suspended from work. Compared with the other two curriculum groups, the High/Scope group reported more of its members voting in the past presidential election.

By contrast, in comparison with just each other, neither the High/Scope group nor the Nursery School group shows a clear pattern of advantages at age 23. On one hand, the High/Scope group has the advantage just mentioned regarding voting and one other important advantage — a lower mean rank on acts of misconduct reported at age 23. The Nursery School group, on the other hand, has had fewer years of compensatory education and reports higher average annual earnings.

This study supports the idea that early childhood programs in which children initiate their own learning activities are superior to programs based on teacher-directed instruction. Further, it identifies the High/Scope Curriculum and a traditional Nursery School curriculum as particular methods that are effective in helping children to make decisions, solve problems, and get along with others — and in the long run, to avoid crime.

LASTING DIFFERENCES

I Curriculum Comparison

The age-27 findings of the High/Scope Perry Preschool Project confirmed that a high-quality program for young children living in poverty can cut their later crime rate in half, improve their school success and economic productivity, and return taxpayers over seven dollars for every dollar invested (Barnett, 1996; Schweinhart, Barnes, & Weikart, 1993). In light of these findings, the question of which preschool curriculum model or models have such beneficial effects takes on considerable significance. Preschool teachers have an obligation not only to maintain children's immediate well-being but also to prepare children for the life that stretches before them. Determining which curriculum models have lasting benefits is a first step in meeting this obligation, and for this we turn to curriculum comparison studies like the one that is the subject of this monograph.

The High/Scope Preschool Curriculum Comparison Study Through Age 23

David P. Weikart and his colleagues began the High/Scope Preschool Curriculum Comparison Study in 1967 to compare the effects of three diverse preschool curriculum models on young children living in poverty. Chosen for comparison were the High/Scope, Direct Instruction, and traditional Nursery School curriculum models—three theoretically distinct approaches to early learning and development. Project staff employed a stratified random assignment procedure to assign each of 68 three- and four-year-old children living in poverty in Ypsilanti, Michigan, to one of the three curriculum models. Each child remained in the assigned model for 1 or 2 school years, depending on whether entry was at age 4 or age 3, respectively. Program staff implemented each of the curriculum models independently and according to the highest standards. The children in each model attended 2½-hour classes 5 days a week and, with their parents, received biweekly 1½-hour home visits. Except for the curriculum model differences, all aspects of the three programs (such as hours of operation, staff-child ratio, and resources) were identical.

Through age 10, the major curriculum-group difference on intellectual performance tests was that, compared with the Nursery School group, the Direct Instruction group had a significantly higher mean IQ on the Stanford-Binet Intelligence Test (Terman & Merrill, 1960) at the end of the preschool program (age 5) but not subsequently (Weikart, Epstein, Schweinhart, & Bond, 1978). This difference of 11 points, however, was less than the end-of-preschool mean-IQ increase for each of the curriculum groups — 24 points for the Direct Instruction group, 19 points for the High/Scope group, and 14 points for the Nursery School group.[1] Consequently, the conclusion at that time was that one well-implemented preschool curriculum model had about the same effect as another on children's intellectual and academic performance.

---

[1]These numbers, as presented in Table 5 on p. 36, differ from those presented in previous reports because of variations in the cases included.

Quite a different picture, however, emerged from the study findings through age 15, when the outcomes to be measured expanded to include community behavior as well as intellectual and academic performance (Schweinhart, Weikart, & Larner, 1986b). At age 15 the Direct Instruction group reported committing significantly more acts of misconduct than the High/Scope group — indeed, over two-and-a-half times as many.[2] In addition, at age 15 the Direct Instruction group evidenced significantly less occupational knowledge (on the Adult APL Survey [American College Testing Program, 1976]) than the High/Scope group, had fewer members appointed to a school job or class office than the Nursery School group, were not as well thought of by their families as the other two curriculum groups, and had fewer members engaged in sports than the other two groups had.

The discovery of these differential curriculum effects at age 15 served as the impetus, and also as the primary source of hypotheses, for the study through age 23. Were these age-15 findings accidental, somehow due to the study's methodological limitations? Direct Instruction proponents believed that they were (Bereiter, 1986; Gersten, 1986). In defense of Direct Instruction, they raised a series of methodological issues, to which Schweinhart, Weikart, and Larner (1986a) responded. This monograph's description of the methodology of this study, in Chapter 2, identifies and responds to these issues as well. In particular, although delinquency researchers have for years routinely used data from self-report (e.g., review by Hindelang, Hirschi, & Weis, 1981), the critics challenged the validity of this study's self-reported misconduct. This study through age 23 includes an examination of actual public arrest records.

Some critics have raised basic questions about objectivity, asking whether the empirical study of the effects of curriculum models is properly carried out by curriculum developers. Traditionally, curriculum developers have had the strongest motivation to conduct comparative studies and have been in a good position to exercise quality control over curriculum implementation, but they also are open to criticism of having a vested interest in the results. The challenge, then, is to build into a study adequate safeguards against subjective biases, which is something that any scientist does who wants fair tests of study hypotheses. These safeguards must be presented for public scrutiny — much as the decisions of a sports referee, who might prefer one team over the other, are subjected to the immediate and widespread scrutiny of an audience. In the study reported in this monograph, the principal investigators were not neutral, but they made every effort to conduct all aspects of the study without bias. Readers concerned about the objectivity of the study should examine the safeguards against bias presented in Chapter 2. The validity and fairness of this study are critical to its ability to determine what is best for young children.

The initial research question and design of this curriculum comparison study were natural consequences of the initial research question and design of the High/Scope Perry Preschool Project (Weikart, Deloria, Lawser, & Wiegerink, 1970), which immediately preceded it. The High/Scope Perry study employed an experimental group and a control group to assess whether a high-quality early childhood program is better for young chil-

---

[2]The number of acts of misconduct reported at age 15 is based on a recalibration of the variable presented earlier by Schweinhart et al. (1986b). See Table 11, footnote *a*.

dren living in poverty than no program at all. It ultimately found that such a program, using the High/Scope Curriculum, improved children's early childhood intellectual performance, later school achievement, high school graduation rate, and adult earnings; cut their lifetime arrest rate in half; and returned $7.16 to taxpayers for every dollar invested (Schweinhart et al., 1993).

The High/Scope Preschool Curriculum Comparison Study, as originally designed in 1967, employed a three-curriculum-group design to ask how effective *various* early childhood curriculum models are for young children living in poverty. Ultimately, in light of the age-27 findings of the Perry Project, it ended up asking if the High/Scope model was an essential part of the high-quality preschool program that produced dramatic lifetime results — or if other curriculum models could just as well have been substituted. Just as the Perry study assessed the value of high-quality early childhood education, so did the High/Scope Preschool Curriculum Comparison Study assess how broadly high-quality early childhood education should be defined — whether it should encompass radically different definitions of early childhood education, definitions built on differing theoretical bases. Fortunately, because the study participants in the two studies were selected using the same criteria of low socioeconomic status and intellectual performance at study entry, it was possible to make close comparisons between the two studies' outcome variables.

When a study compares three curriculum models, with respect to any given outcome variable there can be many patterns of results: The study can demonstrate that all three models are equally effective; that two of them are more effective than the third; that one of them is more effective than one or two of the others; or that none of them are effective. The general conclusions from the age-10 and age-15 findings of the High/Scope Preschool Curriculum Comparison Study are that (a) at the end of the preschool program, all three models were highly effective in improving school performance, with the Direct Instruction program having a temporary significant 11-point edge over the Nursery School program and (b) the High/Scope model was significantly better than the Direct Instruction model in preventing misconduct (self-reported) through age 15. Thus, the leading hypothesis of the study through age 23 was that the High/Scope group would evidence significantly less antisocial behavior (misconduct and crime) than the Direct Instruction group.

A Survey of Early Childhood Curriculum Comparison Studies

The study reported in this monograph stands at the beginning of a collection of studies examining the relative merits of various early childhood curriculum models. Some of these studies have been *intensive* — internally valid and meaningful because they had strict experimental designs, but hard to generalize because they were at single sites and conducted with 500 or fewer children (Schweinhart, 1994). Examples are the High/Scope Preschool Curriculum Comparison Study reported here and two other preschool curriculum comparison studies, one conducted at the University of Louisville and the other at the University of Illinois (these latter two studies are further described below). Other comparison studies have been *extensive* — easy to generalize because they were conducted at multiple sites and with over 500 children, but of questionable internal validity and meaning because of their less strict, quasi-experimental designs.

One example of the ambiguities inherent in extensive studies is a study of 9,859 Seattle youngsters (Sanders & Haynes, 1985; summarized by Schweinhart & Mazur, 1987). This study found that compared with a group of children from regular Head Start programs and with a no-preschool-program group, significantly more (81%) of those from Direct Instruction preschool programs continued to stay on grade for their age (the corresponding Head Start and no-program percentages were 72% and 70%, respectively). The same relative pattern applied regarding the percentages of the three groups that had been assigned to gifted classes. Also, significantly fewer (11%) from the Direct Instruction group dropped out of high school (compared with 17% of the no-preschool-program group and 14% of the regular Head Start group). However, in this study, because children were not randomly assigned to groups, selection bias was clearly a problem: Overall, two thirds of the families in the study were low-income, but the Head Start group had significantly more children from low-income families and single-parent families than did the other two groups. Thus, the differences in outcomes across the three groups may have been due to an uneven distribution of participants from low-income families rather than to differences in programs.

Three Intensive Long-Term Comparison Studies

The **High/Scope Preschool Curriculum Comparison Study** has not been the only intensive, long-term study to look at the Direct Instruction and traditional Nursery School models. These two models were also part of the **University of Louisville Study of Head Start** (Miller & Bizzell, 1983; Miller & Dyer, 1975) and the **University of Illinois Study** (Karnes, Schwedel, & Williams, 1983; Karnes, Teska, & Hodgins, 1970), both of which, like the High/Scope study, began in the 1960s. The children in the Louisville and Illinois studies attended preschool programs for 1 year, while most of the children in the High/Scope study attended preschool programs for 2 years. All three studies collected a variety of measures of intellectual performance from children and later joined the Consortium for Longitudinal Studies and collected interview and records data. Besides the Direct Instruction and traditional Nursery School models, the Louisville and Illinois studies included additional models (not the High/Scope model, however).[3] This report discusses primarily those comparisons involving the models that all three

[3]The Louisville study also included groups using the Montessori model (Montessori, 1964) and the DARCEE model of academic small-group instruction (Gray, Klaus, Miller, & Forrester, 1966); the Illinois study also included groups using the Montessori model, the highly

of these studies had in common — Direct Instruction and Nursery School.

All three intensive studies found that children in Direct Instruction programs initially outperformed children in traditional and other programs on various measures of intellectual performance, but these significant differences appeared only during the preschool program or no more than a year afterward. In the Louisville study, the Direct Instruction group's mean IQ peaked at 98 and dropped 11 points by the end of second grade, while the traditional program group's mean IQ peaked at 96 and dropped 6 points (Miller & Dyer, 1975). In the Illinois study, the Direct Instruction group's mean IQ peaked at 114 and dropped 23 points by age 16; the traditional program group's mean IQ peaked at 102 and dropped 12 points by age 16 (Karnes et al., 1983). In the High/Scope study, the Direct Instruction group peaked at 108 and dropped 10 points by age 10, while the Nursery School group peaked at 102 and dropped 11 points by age 10. Thus, all three studies confirmed that the widely observed pattern regarding preschool program effect — initial IQ improvement followed by later fade-out — applies to the Direct Instruction and Nursery School models. The High/Scope study also found fade-out with the High/Scope model — the High/Scope group peaked at 106 and dropped 10 points by age 10 (when the mean IQ was nonetheless 19 points higher than at study entry).

The Illinois and Louisville studies had additional findings unique to each. In the Louisville study, during the preschool programs, both Direct Instruction and traditional program children scored below other-program and comparison children on a measure of inventiveness (deciding how many ways a dog can get to a bone). The traditional program children showed higher verbal-social participation and increased more in ambition and aggressiveness than did Direct Instruction children. However, no significant inter-group differences were found at seventh and eighth grades.

In the Illinois study, Direct Instruction children's achievement test scores were significantly higher than those of traditional program children at the end of first grade and at the end of second grade, but not at the end of third grade (when achievement test items begin to require more-complex problem solving) or at any time thereafter through the end of high school. Nonetheless, the study found the high school graduation rates to be noticeably different — 70% for the traditional program group, 48% for the Direct Instruction group, and 47% for the no-program group.

More Recent Curriculum Comparison Studies

A good deal of additional early childhood curriculum comparison research has been conducted since the High/Scope study reported its results through age 15 (Schweinhart et al., 1986b). Kagan and Zigler (1987) and Rescorla, Hyson, and Hirsh-Pasek (1991) have edited volumes that capture the debate. Some of the notable studies are these:

---

structured Ameliorative model (Karnes, Zehrbach, & Teska, 1972), and the Community-Integrated model. The Illinois study examined the original Direct Instruction class developed and occasionally taught by Siegfried Engelmann.

- **Burts, Charlesworth, Hart, and their associates** (Burts, Hart, Charlesworth, & Kirk, 1990; Burts et al., 1992; Charlesworth et al., 1993) have engaged in a program of intensive research based on assessing teachers' developmentally appropriate beliefs and practices as defined by the National Association for the Education of Young Children (NAEYC; Bredekamp, 1987) and related child outcomes. (In their research, "developmentally appropriate practice" corresponds to the High/Scope and Nursery School models in the study reported in this monograph, while "developmentally inappropriate practice" corresponds to the Direct Instruction model.) Examining a sample of 37 kindergarten children, they found that those in a developmentally inappropriate class exhibited significantly more stress behaviors (complaints of feeling sick, stuttering, fights, tremors, nervous laughter, nail biting) than did those in a developmentally appropriate class (Burts et al., 1990). Upon replicating this finding with a sample of 204 kindergarten children, they found these curriculum-group differences to be most pronounced for males and for African-American children (Burts et al., 1992). They also confirmed that their questionnaire produces reliable factors of teacher beliefs that relate, as predicted, to their practices (Charlesworth et al., 1993).
- Comparative curriculum research is important to the extent that the curriculum models compared represent the choices actually made by early childhood teachers. Working on this principle, **Marcon** (1992, 1994) identified three different preschool models operating in the public schools of Washington, D.C.—teacher-directed, child-initiated, and "middle-of-the-road" — and examined the development of a random sample of 295 children attending these types of programs. (In terms of the study reported in this monograph, the "teacher-directed" programs resembled Direct Instruction, and the "child-initiated" programs resembled High/Scope.) Children from the various types of classes differed significantly in their mastery of basic reading, language, and mathematics skills, with children from child-initiated classes showing the greatest mastery of these skills, followed first by children from teacher-directed classes and then by children from "middle-of-the-road" classes (Marcon, 1992). Although not statistically significant, this same ranking of curriculum types appeared at fourth grade on children's grade-point averages overall and in most subject matter areas (Marcon, 1994).
- Additional evidence that the curriculum approaches examined in the study reported in this monograph are widespread comes from an analysis of detailed observations of 62 preschool and kindergarten classes in the Los Angeles area by **Stipek, Daniels, Galluzzo, and Milburn** (1992). They empirically identified three types of programs — didactic programs focusing on academics in a negative social context, child-centered programs deemphasizing academics in a positive social context, and intermediate programs between these two extremes. They found no examples of another logical possibility — didactic programs focusing on academics in a positive social context.
- In the Academic Environments study, **Hirsh-Pasek, Hyson, and Rescorla** (1990) studied ninety 4- and 5-year-olds in a variety of academic

and child-centered preschool programs in affluent areas of Philadelphia and Delaware and followed 56 of them through the end of kindergarten. They found that *preschool program type* had no significant influence on children's academic or logical skills at the end of kindergarten. But then, other studies have found few effects of any sort of preschool program on children from affluent families (Hauser-Cram, Pierson, Walker, & Tivnan, 1991; Larsen, Hite, Hart, & Robinson, 1994; Larsen & Robinson, 1989).

- In the High/Scope Training of Trainers Evaluation, **Epstein** (1993) compared preschool classes having teachers who were High/Scope-trained with other high-quality, non-High/Scope classes. She verified that the average teacher-trainer participating successfully in a High/Scope Training of Trainers program learned how to conduct workshops that actively involve participants, improve programs through observation-based advice, and overcome barriers to change. When compared with the preschool programs of teachers not trained by these trainers, the programs of teachers trained by these trainers were rated significantly higher in classroom arrangement; in enabling children to plan, carry out, and review their own activities; and in their use of adult-child interaction to promote children's reasoning and language skills. Compared with children in nominated high-quality classes not using the High/Scope Curriculum, children in the High/Scope classes rated significantly higher at the end of the school year in their initiative, social relations, music and movement skills, and overall development.
- In another study of the effects of the High/Scope Curriculum, **Frede and Barnett** (1992) found that preschool programs throughout South Carolina implementing the High/Scope Curriculum moderately to very well contributed more to children's school achievement at kindergarten and first-grade entry than did programs with low implementation levels.

Two Extensive Comparison Studies

One well-known extensive preschool study, the **Planned Variation Head Start Project,** ran from 1969 to 1972 and was Head Start's version of the Office of Education's early elementary Follow Through Project, which had begun earlier, in 1967. The evaluation of Planned Variation Head Start included a dozen preschool curriculum models at 37 sites across the country with some 6,000 children enrolled in model programs (Bissell, 1971; Datta, McHale, & Mitchell, 1976; Smith, 1973; Weisberg, 1973). The dozen models to be evaluated included the Direct Instruction model, the High/Scope model, and the "Enabler model," which was guided by early childhood consultants specializing in the traditional Nursery School model. Study participants, although in Head Start, were heterogeneous in family socioeconomic status and initial intellectual performance. Studies of this size are usually fraught with design problems, and this one was no exception. Nonetheless, two clear findings emerged.

- At the end of the preschool program, children in Direct Instruction and other programmed-learning programs had the highest achievement test scores of all the program and comparison groups.
- Of all the program and comparison groups, children in High/Scope programs had the greatest gains in intellectual performance. Their average gain on the Stanford-Binet Intelligence Scale was 23 points; this compared with at most a 5-point average gain for children in other models.[4]

Another example of an extensive comparison study, the **Follow Through Project** we have already mentioned, was intended to provide children who had attended Head Start with the kindergarten-through-third-grade "follow through" needed to avoid the presumed fade-out of Head Start effects (Zigler & Muenchow, 1992). During its existence from 1967 to 1995, Follow Through never went beyond its initial demonstration status — that is to say, it never involved more than a small fraction of the nation's children who had attended Head Start. The project did, however, serve as a development and proving ground for a variety of 20 early elementary curriculum models, including the Direct Instruction and High/Scope models. The national evaluation also produced findings about the relative effects of these curriculum models (Stebbins, St. Pierre, Proper, Anderson, & Cerva, 1977). One of Follow Through's general conclusions was that program outcomes varied more across sites than across curriculum models. But the Follow Through project did not and could not answer the more basic question, the one addressed by the High/Scope Preschool Curriculum Comparison Study reported here: Which curriculum model, when carried out as intended under ideal conditions, is most effective in achieving its declared objectives — and in achieving the widely agreed-upon objectives for early childhood programs? If a curriculum model proves to be effective under ideal circumstances, then its relative ineffectiveness in other circumstances may be due to less-than-ideal implementation.

What the Follow Through evaluation *did* find concerning curriculum comparison was this: Compared with their peers in regular elementary school programs, during the early years of Follow Through, Direct Instruction students did significantly better on school achievement tests and also on measures of self-esteem and achievement responsibility (Stebbins et al., 1977). A decade later, in each of four selected sites, Direct Instruction researchers compared former Direct Instruction students with students from an elementary school that was comparable in ethnicity and percentage of families receiving welfare assistance (Gersten & Keating, 1987). However, without random assignment to groups and more-detailed information on study participants' background characteristics, it is impossible to say with certainty that observed outcome differences between any two groups of students were due to differences in educational models rather than to differences in group composition. This caution needs to be kept in mind when considering that the former Direct Instruction students signifi-

[4]The High/Scope Foundation is now completing a 20-year follow-up study of the study participants at the High/Scope sites where these results occurred.

cantly outperformed comparison students at specifically selected sites in the following ways:

- At two of the four sites, the Direct Instruction students had a higher rate of high school graduation (60% vs. 38% at a site in New York City — Meyer, 1984).
- At three of the four sites, the Direct Instruction students scored higher on ninth-grade achievement tests.
- At two of the four sites, the Direct Instruction students repeated fewer grades.
- At one of the four sites, the Direct Instruction students had a lower rate of absenteeism — fewer students with 10 or more school absences per year.

Unlike the Direct Instruction model, the High/Scope elementary school model aims not only to improve children's achievement test scores but also to develop their initiative, social relations, and creative skills — outcomes that achievement tests do not measure. Unlike the Direct Instruction students, in the early years of Follow Through, High/Scope students did not score significantly better on achievement tests when compared with their peers in typical elementary school programs (Stebbins et al., 1977). However, later in the Follow Through Project, in 1988–91, High/Scope classes in three schools scored significantly higher than comparison classes in the same or similar schools on 22 of 40 composite-score comparisons of school achievement; on none of the 40 comparisons did High/Scope classes score significantly lower. The average High/Scope advantage was 13.2 normal-curve-equivalent points (Schweinhart & Wallgren, 1993). This evidence suggests that in recent years, High/Scope classes have improved school achievement more effectively than have typical elementary school classes serving similar children.

How does one account for the apparent superiority of Direct Instruction on improving achievement test scores in the early years of Follow Through? There could have been selection bias between Follow Through and comparison groups within sites as well as across the sites at which various models were practiced (House, Glass, McLean, & Walker, 1978). Children were not randomly assigned, and comparison schools, who voluntarily participated, served as no more than rough matches. Yet, this design flaw is probably not a complete explanation of Direct Instruction's success. A more persuasive explanation is that achievement tests naturally favor Direct Instruction (Kennedy, 1978), since the sole purpose of Direct Instruction is to improve children's achievement test scores. Also, Direct Instruction may work better at the elementary level than at the preschool level. Being at a higher developmental stage, elementary school children may be better able to follow its strict rules of behavior and its logic of mastery learning; and elementary school teachers may more fully embrace its methods than do preschool teachers (many of whom consider it developmentally inappropriate), and hence the elementary school teachers may implement the model with greater fidelity and enthusiasm.

A Survey of Curriculum Comparison Studies Addressing Antisocial Behavior

Of particular interest to us as we pursued the High/Scope Preschool Curriculum Comparison Study through age 23 was a survey of curriculum comparison studies with findings that relate to antisocial behavior. (Recall that the leading hypothesis at this stage of the study was that the High/Scope group at age 23 would evidence significantly less antisocial behavior than the Direct Instruction group.) The question had become this: How can a preschool curriculum prevent antisocial behavior and crime? The simplest hypothesis would be that the preschool curriculum helps to prevent antisocial behavior immediately and that reduced antisocial behavior becomes an enduring habit culminating in a lower crime rate. However, antisocial behavior is not an isolated trait, so a preschool curriculum that reduces antisocial behavior should also affect other habits that are intimately related to reduced antisocial behavior. Examination of differences in various curriculum models' objectives suggests that two types of related habits are involved — sociomoral action and reasoning, and planning ability.

Sociomoral Action and Reasoning

DeVries and associates found that children experiencing constructivist education in preschool evidence better *sociomoral action and reasoning* than do children experiencing Direct Instruction in preschool (DeVries, Haney, & Zan, 1991; DeVries, Reese-Learned, & Morgan, 1991). They systematically observed three kindergarten classes — one used Direct Instruction, another used a constructivist approach like High/Scope's, and the third was eclectic. Analyzing teachers' interactions with children, they found that the constructivist *teacher* significantly surpassed the other two in her use of reciprocal and collaborative negotiation strategies and shared experiences. They found that during two game-like activities, the *children* from the constructivist class were more interpersonally interactive, demonstrated a greater number and variety of negotiation strategies, and had more shared experiences than children from the other two classes. DeVries (1991) offered an explanation of her results that apply, by extension, to the findings of this study:

> When we unilaterally focus on giving children information, we are also communicating "lessons" about human relations. In the process we are creating the context for construction of interpersonal habits, personality, and character. Our study (DeVries, Reese-Learned, & Morgan, 1991) suggests that when children experience a heavily unilateral atmosphere, their sociomoral action and underlying reasoning are less advanced than when children experience a more reciprocal atmosphere. (p. 546)

We believe that these differences in sociomoral action and reasoning in early childhood (identified by DeVries and her associates) serve as correlates of antisocial behavior in early childhood and as antecedents of antisocial behavior and crime in early adulthood.

Planning Ability

In addition to this sociomoral dimension, *planning ability* — or the lack of it — also hypothetically serves as a mediator between preschool curriculum and later antisocial behavior. In the High/Scope program and, to a lesser extent, in the Nursery School program, adults encourage children to select and plan their own activities, to be decision-makers to the extent that their ages and abilities permit. Their habits of considered decision-making lead to more disciplined behavior in early childhood and then later in adulthood. Early childhood education can help children develop their ability to make plans (Bronson, 1994), and this ability has been found to be a factor in school achievement (Cohen, Bronson, & Casey, 1995). Linking planning ability to crime prevention, many effective correctional programs have an emphasis on participants' critical thinking and reasoning about their behavior (Andrews et al., 1990; Antonowicz & Ross, 1994).

The evidence that sociomoral action and reasoning and planning ability are mediators in the High/Scope Preschool Curriculum Comparison Study comes mainly from analysis of the programs themselves. Assessment of children's behavior did not focus squarely on antisocial behavior, sociomoral habits, or planning ability. However, at first grade, teacher ratings of the curriculum groups in elementary school revealed a nonsignificant tendency for the High/Scope group to be rated as more cooperative than the Direct Instruction group, and at second grade, the Nursery School group was rated as significantly more independent than the Direct Instruction group (Weikart et al., 1978). These slight differences may have been precursors to later group differences in antisocial behavior and crime.

The weight of the evidence from other studies favors child-centered, constructivist preschool classes over Direct Instruction preschool classes. The question is whether a similar outcome pattern will prevail in this study.

II Methodology

The High/Scope Preschool Curriculum Comparison Study began with a sample of 68 three-year-olds who lived in families of low socioeconomic status and had low scores on the Stanford-Binet Intelligence Scale. The children were assigned to three curriculum groups — High/Scope, Direct Instruction, and Nursery School — by a random-assignment procedure that matched groups on race, gender, and mean socioeconomic status of family. The three curriculum groups were comparable on most background characteristics in the full sample at program entry, in the subsample interviewed at age 23, and in the subsample whose school records were found. On two background characteristics at age 23, the Nursery School group was significantly different from the High/Scope group: The Nursery School group had fewer African-American children and had mothers with a higher level of schooling. Also, more Direct Instruction group members than Nursery School group members were living in Ypsilanti when interviewed at age 23.

Staff operated all three programs according to the same high standards of quality — each program had 2 teachers with up to 16 children, educational home visits every other week, daily evaluation and planning, and strong and consistent curriculum supervision and training. Each program, however, employed a different curriculum model — either Direct Instruction, High/Scope, or traditional Nursery School. Data on sample members were collected annually at ages 3 through 8 and at ages 10, 15, and 23. For this data collection, researchers employed various tests of intelligence, language ability, school achievement, and literacy. Sample members were also interviewed at ages 15 and 23; in addition, school records and arrest records were collected at age 23. The principal techniques of data analysis were chi-square analysis and one-way analysis of variance, supplemented by two-way analysis of variance and the Kruskal-Wallis analysis of mean ranks.

Sample Selection

As previously described (Weikart et al., 1978; Schweinhart et al., 1986b), the study sample consisted of 68 children who lived in Ypsilanti, Michigan; turned 3 years old in 1967, 1968, or 1969; lived in families of low socioeconomic status; and scored low on the Stanford-Binet Intelligence Scale (Terman & Merrill, 1960) at age 3. (See insert on p. 16.)

The census of the Ypsilanti Public Schools was used to identify the pool from which children were selected for the study. Sample members were born in 1964, 1965, or 1966; attended the preschool programs at ages 3 and 4 (from 1967 through 1970); and completed age-10 interviews in 1974 through 1976, age-15 interviews in 1979 through 1981, and age-23 interviews in 1987 through 1989.[5] In September of the year that each of these children turned

---

[5]As in the age-15 study (Schweinhart et al., 1986b), the first, second, and third cohorts employed in this age-23 study correspond, respectively, to Waves Five, Six, and Seven in the original report (Weikart et al., 1978); the fourth cohort, called Wave Eight, was excluded from the age-15 study and from this study because, though the Wave Eight children experienced the study's three different curriculum models at age 3, they all experienced only the High/Scope model at age 4.

age 3, school district staff asked the children's parents to complete a questionnaire identifying (a) *parental occupation* (the occupation of the father in two-parent families or of the only parent in single-parent families was coded from 1 to 5, as unemployed [1], unskilled [2], semiskilled [3], skilled [4], or professional [5]); (b) *parents' highest year of schooling* (this was the highest year completed by the mother in single-parent families or the mean of the highest years completed by both parents); and (c) *number of rooms per person in the household.* Since the parents who *were* employed had unskilled jobs, the occupation measure yielded a score of unemployed (1) or unskilled (2). A data analyst divided the scores on each of the three measures by the sample's standard deviation on that measure to give the three factors equal weighting. The transformed rooms-per-person score was then divided by 2 to give it half the weight of the other two factors. Families scoring a total of 11 or less on the *occupation, schooling,* and *rooms-per-person* measures were judged to be living in poverty and eligible for the study sample.

Next, the 3-year-olds in these "poverty" families completed the Stanford-Binet Intelligence Scale (Form L-M; Terman & Merrill, 1960). Children scoring between 60 and 90 and with no evidence of physical disability were admitted to the study sample, for which the mean IQ at age 3 was 78. On this basis, these children at age 3 might have been classified as slow learners, at risk of school failure. (It will be noted later, however, that by the time sample children entered school, their preschool program experience had essentially erased this classification: 82% of them had an IQ of 85 or lower at the *beginning* of their preschool programs, but only 16% of them had an IQ of 85 or lower at the *end* of their preschool programs.)

These criteria of low family socioeconomic status and low intellectual performance at study entry were precisely the same as the criteria for

Ypsilanti — Setting for the Study

Ypsilanti, in the late 1960s, had a population of 29,538 — 20% African-American (U.S. Bureau of the Census, 1972). Situated about 30 miles west of Detroit and with several automobile plants in the immediate area, the small city was (and still is) very much a part of the automobile industry of southeastern Michigan. Ypsilanti is also the home of a community college, a business college, and Eastern Michigan University, while its neighbor city, Ann Arbor, is the home of the University of Michigan. The median income of Ypsilanti residents in 1969 was $10,710, with 27% living in poverty (the poverty threshold for a non-farm family of four in 1969 was $3,743); for African-American adults in Ypsilanti, the median income in 1969 was $3,785. At that time, the adult population of Ypsilanti had completed a median 12.2 years of schooling, and 54% had graduated from high school; for Ypsilanti's African-Americans, the median length of schooling was 10.1 years, and 31% had graduated from high school.

High/Scope Perry Preschool Project participants (Weikart et al., 1970). The major difference between the two samples is that the High/Scope Perry Preschool Project participants were *all* African-Americans who lived in the neighborhood of the Perry Elementary School on the South Side of Ypsilanti, whereas only 65% of the Curriculum Comparison Study participants were African-Americans, and sample members lived throughout the city of Ypsilanti.

Several children in the Comparison Study's initial sample pool were already attending other early childhood programs, so their parents declined to have them participate in the study. Several others eventually dropped out of the study's three preschool programs because their families moved out of the district. Two children, after initial selection, were later (in the data analysis) judged ineligible for the study because their parents' socioeconomic level had risen considerably past the poverty level.

The children who met the entry criteria and completed the preschool programs — a total of 68 — served as the original study sample. The oldest class (first cohort) had 27 children in it; the next-oldest (second cohort) had 19; and the youngest (third cohort) had 22. As the *all programs* column in Table 1 on page 20 shows, the original study sample had the following characteristics:

- 65% were African-American, and 35% were White.
- 54% were females, and 46% were males.
- 32% of the children lived in single-parent families, and 68% lived in two-parent families.
- 98% of the children in the two-parent families had fathers who were employed outside the home.
- 33% of the children had mothers who were employed outside the home.
- Fathers on average had completed grade 9.
- Mothers on average had completed grade 10.
- Households averaged 6.7 residents, 1.1 per room.

As Table 2 on p. 21 and Table 3 on p. 23 show, the 52 sample members interviewed at age 23 had characteristics that were quite similar to those of the original study sample. In addition, they had the following characteristics:

- As reported by *respondents* at age 23, fathers on average had completed half of grade 12 (as compared with an average of grade 9, as reported by the *parents* of the original sample at project entry 20 years earlier).
- As reported by *respondents* at age 23, mothers on average had completed two fifths of grade 12 (as compared with an average of grade 10, as reported by the *parents* of the original sample at project entry 20 years earlier).

- Three fourths of the age-23 sample members (39 of them) were interviewed in their home; of the rest, 5 were interviewed at their mother's home, 2 were interviewed in jail, 2 were interviewed at local universities, and 1 each was interviewed at a boyfriend's home, a sister's home, a laundromat, and the High/Scope Foundation offices.
- Sample members were interviewed at an average age of 23½
- 65% of the age-23 sample members were living in Ypsilanti, 10% were living elsewhere in Washtenaw County, 12% were living elsewhere in Michigan, and 12% were living elsewhere in the U.S.

Assignment to Curriculum Groups

Staff randomly assigned the children in each of three annual cohorts to three separate groups. They then reassigned them from one group to another until each group had about the same percentages of Blacks and Whites, percentages of boys and girls, and mean Stanford-Binet IQ. (For achieving comparable groups in small-sample research, this group-matching technique is probably superior to simple random assignment.) Finally, each of the three groups was randomly assigned to one of the curriculum models — a Direct Instruction class, a High/Scope class, or a Nursery School class. To avoid confounding the effects of different curriculum models within any one family, 9 of the 68 children were reassigned so they would experience the same curriculum model as an older sibling; this, in effect, changed the sampling units from *children* to *families*.

In the first cohort,

- The High/Scope class was selected at age 3 and experienced the High/Scope Curriculum at ages 3 and 4.
- The Direct Instruction class spent its age-3 year as a comparison group that did not attend a preschool program and its age-4 year in the Direct Instruction program.
- The Nursery School class was not a part of the study and did not attend a preschool program during its age-3 year; it was selected and attended the Nursery School program at age 4.

Thus, in this first cohort only, curriculum model was confounded with program duration. However, other research, then and now, has suggested that a second preschool-program year adds little to the effects of one preschool-program year (Reynolds, 1995; Weikart et al., 1970), and no evidence of program duration effects has been found in this High/Scope Preschool Curriculum Comparison Study (Schweinhart et al., 1986b). Because the first-cohort High/Scope ($n = 11$) and Direct Instruction ($n = 8$) classes were also part of the all-African-American design of the High/Scope Perry Preschool Project, all of the children in these two classes were African-American. Of the 8 children in the first-cohort Nursery School class, 4 were African-American and 4 were White. This first-cohort pattern explains why, despite the matching of the three classes on race in the second and third cohorts, the High/Scope group had the most African-Americans, followed by the Direct Instruction group, then the Nursery School group.

To summarize, one subgroup of the first annual cohort attended the High/Scope program at ages 3 and 4, while the other subgroups attended the Direct Instruction and Nursery School programs at age 4 only. The second and third annual cohorts attended the three programs at both age 3 and age 4. In each program each school year, 3-year-olds from one cohort attended with 4-year-olds from the previous cohort. An additional cohort of children at the end of the study was not included in the study sample; these children attended the three different programs at age 3 but only the High/Scope program at age 4.

Comparability of the Curriculum Groups

As Table 1 (on p. 20) shows, regarding background characteristics at program entry, the three curriculum groups did not differ significantly (p less than .05, two-tailed) or nearly significantly (p between .05 and .10) on race (African-American vs. White), gender (male vs. female), mean socioeconomic status of family, single-parent versus two-parent family, father's employment rate, mother's employment rate, father's highest year of schooling, persons per household, persons per room, or child's mean Stanford-Binet IQ. However, mothers of the Nursery School group, on average, attended school significantly longer than the High/Scope-group mothers — a difference that would serve as a bias *against* finding advantages for the High/Scope group over the Nursery School group. Examination of mother's highest year of schooling combined with father's highest year of schooling reveals how this occurred despite the use of *parents' highest year of schooling* as a selection criterion. Using the formula employed for sample selection — where *parents' highest year of schooling* was defined as the average of mother's and father's highest years of schooling or the single parent's highest year of schooling — the curriculum groups did not differ significantly on parents' highest year of schooling; the relevant means were 9.4 for the Direct Instruction group, 9.5 for the High/Scope group, and 9.8 for the Nursery School group. This counterbalance is an argument against attaching undue importance to the significant difference in mother's highest year of schooling.

Table 2 presents the results of a two-way analysis of variance of background variables, using *curriculum group* and *interview-status* (whether sample members were interviewed at age 23) as the main factors. This analysis asked whether the curriculum groups differed significantly from one another in their program-entry characteristics according to whether or not they were interviewed at age 23; any such program-entry-characteristic difference (either across the three subsamples interviewed, or across the three subsamples not interviewed) could suggest a study bias toward the model(s) more favored in the curriculum comparison and against the model(s) less favored in the curriculum comparison. The analysis also asked whether the study participants interviewed at age 23 differed from

Table 1

GROUP COMPARISONS OF BACKGROUND CHARACTERISTICS OF THE ORIGINAL STUDY PARTICIPANTS

Characteristic	Total Sample	Direct Instruction	High/ Scope	Nursery School	*p*
Number of study participants	68	23	22	23	
First cohort	27	8	11	8	
Second cohort	19	7	5	7	
Third cohort	22	8	6	8	
African-Americans	65%	65%	77%	52%	—
Females	54%	52%	59%	52%	—
Family socioeconomic status (*n* = 67)	8.8 (1.1)	8.7 (1.0)	9.0 (1.3)	8.9 (1.0)	—
Single-parent family (*n* = 65)	32%	35%	40%	23%	—
Father employed (*n* = 48)	98%	93%	100%	100%	—
Mother employed (*n* = 66)	33%	44%	25%	29%	—
Father's highest year of schooling (*n* = 51)	9.0 (2.2)	9.2 (1.6)	9.6 (1.7)	8.4 (2.9)	—
Mother's highest year of schooling (*n* = 66)	10.0 (1.9)	9.7 (1.7)	9.3* (2.4)	10.9* (1.2)	**.017**
Persons per household (*n* = 65)	6.7 (2.6)	6.8 (2.1)	6.1 (2.5)	7.1 (3.1)	—
Persons per room (*n* = 65)	1.1 (0.4)	1.2 (0.4)	1.0 (0.4)	1.2 (0.4)	—
Child's Stanford-Binet IQ at program entry	78.3 (6.8)	78.8 (7.0)	77.5 (7.0)	78.6 (6.8)	—

Note. Unless otherwise indicated, *n* of the original sample = 68. The chi-square statistic tests differences in percentages; the analysis of variance tests differences in means (followed by standard deviations in parentheses). The associated *p*-value is reported if less than .100. One group value in a row is starred if different from the other two curriculum groups' values at $p < .05$; two group values in a row are starred if different from each other at $p < .05$

*The socioeconomic status scale combines factors of *parental occupation, parental schooling,* and *persons per room.*

the study participants not interviewed at age 23 on background characteristics, either overall (the main *interview-status* effect) or by curriculum group (the *group/interview-status interaction* effect). A main *interview-status* effect means that the interviewed sample members differed significantly from the non-interviewed sample members, while a *group/interview-status interaction* effect means that the interviewed members of certain curriculum groups differed significantly from the non-interviewed members of other curriculum groups.

No significant differences — by *curriculum group,* by *interview status,* or by *interaction* of the two — were found for *gender, family socioeconomic status, single-parent versus two-parent family, mother employed* (the variance in *father employed* could not be analyzed, because 100% of the fathers

Table 2

GROUP COMPARISONS OF PROGRAM-ENTRY CHARACTERISTICS BY AGE-23 INTERVIEW STATUS

Characteristic	Interviewed at Age 23: Total Sample	Direct Inst.	High/ Scope	Nursery School	Curric. Group *p*	Inter-view Status *p*	Group/ Interview-Status Inter-action *p*
***n* of study participants**	52	19	14	19			
First cohort	22	6	9	7			
Second cohort	13	5	2	6			
Third cohort	17	8	3	6			
African-Americans	71%	68%	86%	63%	**.039**	**.013**	—
Females (*n* = 68)	58%	53%	64%	58%	—	—	—
Family socioeconomic status[a] (*n* = 67)	8.8 (1.1)	8.7 (1.1)	8.8 (1.5)	8.8 (1.1)	—	—	—
Single-parent family (*n* = 65)	33%	32%	42%	28%	—	—	—
Father employed (*n* = 48)	100%	100%	100%	100%	—	—	—
Mother employed (*n* = 66)	34%	42%	21%	35%	—	—	.097
Father's highest year of schooling (*n* = 51)	9.3 (2.5)	10.5 (1.9)	9.3 (1.7)	8.7 (3.2)	—	—	—
Mother's highest year of schooling (*n* = 66)	10.0 (2.0)	9.8 (1.7)	9.0 (2.6)	10.8 (1.2)	**.050**	—	—
Persons per household (*n* = 65)	7.1 (2.8)	6.9 (2.2)	6.5 (2.8)	7.6 (3.3)	—	.061	—
Persons per room (*n* = 65)	1.2 (0.4)	1.2 (0.5)	1.1 (0.4)	1.3 (0.4)	—	—	—
Child's Stanford-Binet IQ at program entry	78.2 (7.1)	78.5 (7.1)	78.4 (7.7)	77.8 (7.1)	—	—	—

Note. Unless otherwise indicated, *n* = 68, including both those interviewed at age 23 and those not interviewed. Two-way analyses of variance test differences in means of curriculum groups by age-23 interview status (yes or no) and the interaction between the two, using the unique sums of squares method. The chi-square statistic tests differences in percentages. The associated *p*-value is reported if less than .100.

[a]"Socioeconomic status" combines *mother's* and *father's employment* and *schooling* and *persons per room.*

of the age-23 interviewees were employed), *father's highest year of schooling, persons per room,* or *child's Stanford-Binet IQ at program entry.*

Significant differences were found for the percentage of *African-Americans* by *curriculum group* and by *interview status,* with a nearly significant difference (that is to say, the exact *p* was between .05 and .10) for the *interaction* effect. Comparison of the *total sample* columns in Tables 1 and 2 shows that more of the original Black participants than of the original White participants were found and interviewed at age 23. While 71% (37 out of 52) of the sample members interviewed at age 23 were Blacks, only 65% of the original sample were Blacks. This means that only 44% (7 of 16) of the sample members *not* interviewed at age 23 were Blacks. This difference may have been due to the interviewer's greater familiarity with the Black community (he himself was a Black, lived in the Black community, and found and interviewed 117 of the 123 sample members of the High/Scope Perry Preschool Project, all of whom had come from Ypsilanti's Black community). Or, in the 1970s, Ypsilanti's poor White families may have changed residences more often than Ypsilanti's poor Black families did. Either way, this difference did not affect the comparability of the curriculum groups or the internal validity of the study.

Examination of the percentages of *African-Americans* by *curriculum group* at program entry reveals that the High/Scope group had 77% African-Americans, compared with the Nursery School group's 52% (a 25-point difference) and the Direct Instruction group's 65% (a 12-point difference). At the age-23 interview, the High/Scope group had 86% African-Americans, compared with the Nursery School group's 63% (a 23-point difference) and the Direct Instruction group's 68% (an 18-point difference). Because African-American children suffer the added burden of prejudice against a minority race, the program-entry and age-23 High/Scope groups' higher percentages of African-Americans could indicate a study bias against the High/Scope group. In other words, as compared with the Nursery School program, the High/Scope program probably makes an even greater positive contribution to outcomes than obtained group differences in outcomes would indicate.

Nearly significant group differences ($.05 < p < .10$) were found for the *group/interview-status interaction* effect on *mothers employed* and the *interview-status* effect on *persons per household.* However, the curriculum group statistics on these variables are not very different, and these effects probably did not affect the comparability of the groups or the internal validity of the study.

Curriculum groups differed significantly on *mother's highest year of schooling.* At program entry, *mother's highest year of schooling* for the Nursery School group was 1.6 years higher than that for the High/Scope group and 1.2 years higher than that for the Direct Instruction group — creating a study bias in favor of the Nursery School group.

In summary, only two background variables were significantly different across curriculum groups — *race* and *mother's highest year of schooling.* Differences on both of these variables favored the Nursery School group over the High/Scope group, so outcome differences between the groups probably underestimate the real benefits of the High/Scope program as compared with the Nursery School program.

Another two-way analysis of variance of background variables, like this one, was carried out using *curriculum group* and *school-records status* (records were obtained for 46 sample members) as the main factors. Similar to the findings for *interview status,* the only significant effects were of *curriculum group* and *group-records interaction* on *race,* and of *curriculum group* on *mother's highest year of schooling.* Again, the biases were against the High/Scope group and in favor of the Nursery School group.

Table 3 presents additional background characteristics of the sample members interviewed at age 23. Curriculum groups did not differ signifi-

Table 3

GROUP COMPARISONS OF AGE-23 BACKGROUND CHARACTERISTICS

	Interviewed at Age 23 (n = 52)				
Characteristic	Total Sample	Direct Inst.	High/ Scope	Nursery School	p
Father's highest year of schooling[a] reported by respondent at age 23	11.5 (2.4)	12.3 (3.5)	11.4 (2.3)	10.9 (1.2)	—
Mother's highest year of schooling reported by respondent at age 23	11.4 (1.4)	11.4 (1.7)	11.1 (1.2)	11.5 (1.3)	—
Age at interview (yr)	23.5 (1.1)	23.2 (1.0)	23.7 (0.8)	23.8 (1.4)	—
Interviewed at home[b]	75%	83%	79%	63%	—
Current home (n = 49)					
Ypsilanti	65%	84%*	64%	44%*	.036
Rest of county	10%	5%	0%	25%	
Rest of state	12%	0%	14%	25%	
Rest of U.S.[c]	12%	11%	21%	6%	
Mean rank	*25.0*	*20.6*	*26.4*	*29.0*	—

Note. Unless otherwise indicated, n = 52. The chi-square statistic tests differences in percentages; the analysis of variance tests differences in means (followed by standard deviations in parentheses); the Kruskal-Wallis statistic tests differences in mean ranks. The associated p-value is reported if less than .100. One group value in a row is starred if different from the other two curriculum groups' values at $p < .05$; two group values in a row are starred if different from each other at $p < .05$.

[a]Highest year of schooling is coded as follows: Junior high school = 9; some high school = 10.5; high school graduate or GED = 12; vocational training or community college = 12.5; 1 year of college = 13; 2-year college degree = 14; 2 or more years of college = 15; 4-year college degree = 16; master's degree = 18; doctoral degree = 20.

[b]Interview sites other than homes were mother's home (5 respondents), jail (2), local university (2), boyfriend's home (1), sister's home (1), laundromat (1), and the High/Scope Foundation offices (1).

[c]The 6 respondents residing outside Michigan lived in Alabama, Georgia, Indiana, New York, Pennsylvania, and South Carolina.

cantly on either *mother's* or *father's highest year of schooling* as reported by their children at age 23, despite the curriculum-group differences found on these variables as measured at program entry. Nor did curriculum groups differ on *average age at interview* or the percentages of group members *interviewed at home.*

Curriculum groups did differ significantly in geographic mobility, as indicated in Table 3 by *location of current home.* Only 4 out of every 9 members of the Nursery School group still lived in Ypsilanti, while almost 8 out of every 9 members of the Direct Instruction group still lived in Ypsilanti. Although not statistically significant, similar figures were found for the percentages attending Ypsilanti High School — 83% of the Direct Instruction group, as compared with 69% of the High/Scope group and 39% of the Nursery School group. It seems unlikely that differential geographic mobility before high school is directly attributable to preschool *curriculum model;* it is probably best to treat it as a chance occurrence. Because such differential geographic mobility could have influenced arrest rates by removing (from those study participants living elsewhere) the opportunity to commit crimes and be arrested in their county of origin, special attention will be given to geographic mobility in the analysis of arrest data.

Common Characteristics of Program Operation

This study operated three well-implemented preschool programs that differed only in the curriculum models they employed. All three programs operated in the same context — with the same school administration, director (David P. Weikart), and staff supervisor; the same funding; and the same working conditions and salary schedule for staff. All three programs, throughout three successive school years, had class sessions for children 2½ hours a day Monday through Friday and 1½-hour educational home visits by teachers to each mother and child every other week. Teachers used their respective curriculum models both in the class sessions and in the home visits, and they encouraged parents to use the curriculum model with their children.

The preschool programs were housed in two one-room school buildings located in rural settings away from town. In the study's first year, one building housed the High/Scope class in the morning and the Direct Instruction class in the afternoon, while the other building housed the Nursery School class and the administrative staff. In the subsequent years, the High/Scope and Nursery School classes, which both called for abundant materials and equipment, met in one building, and the Direct Instruction class, which called for an absence of distracting materials and equipment, met in the other. The three classes of children rode to and from their program in separate buses, eliminating contact between the classes.

The classes, which met in the school years between September 1967 and May 1970, typically each had 15 or 16 three- and four-year-olds and a team of 2 certified teachers — a ratio of 1 teacher to about 8 children. The sole exception was the 1969–70 High/Scope class of 13 children (later reduced to 11 by removing, in the analysis, 2 children whose family socioeconomic status grew to greatly exceed the criterion for sample membership). Each classroom had a teaching assistant, who also drove the bus, and a high school special education student, who received school credit for helping with the children, particularly on bus rides and field trips.

In all, 11 different women filled the teaching positions for the classes over the 3 school years. All had a bachelor's degree in education, and most had a master's degree. The same 2 teachers remained with the Nursery School classes throughout all 3 years. The High/Scope and Direct Instruction classes each had 2 new teachers in their second year; the Direct Instruction class also had 1 new teacher in its third year. Each curriculum model had the same teaching assistant throughout all 3 years. All the teachers were highly motivated to prove the success of their curriculum models. See Weikart (1972) for further information about the experiences of individual teachers in the project.

Each teaching team engaged in daily evaluation and planning sessions, focusing on the activities and progress of each child, but the teams from different models never met together. A staff supervisor helped the teaching teams stay focused on their curriculum goals, particularly through her participation in the daily planning and evaluation sessions. Also, after each home visit, the teachers completed home visit reports describing activities and child progress, and they often discussed these reports with the staff supervisor (see Weikart et al., 1978, for an analysis of these reports). The staff supervisor maintained elaborate managerial procedures to help maintain her curriculum neutrality.

The Curriculum Models

The curriculum models used in the study's preschool programs represent three distinct theoretical approaches to early childhood education, three visions of what early childhood education ought to be. As shown in Figure 1, these approaches differ with respect to the degree of initiative expected of the child and the degree of initiative expected of the teacher. Figure 1, which presents a framework developed at the High/Scope Foundation for comparing different approaches to early childhood education, shows curriculum models organized according to whether the child is primarily initiator or respondent and whether the teacher is primarily initiator or respondent (Weikart, 1972, 1974). Similar early childhood approaches were identified by Kohlberg and Mayer (1972) and similar parenting approaches, by Baumrind (1971). In the programmed-learning approach, the child responds to the initiating teacher, while in the child-centered approach, the teacher responds to the initiating child. In the open-framework approach, child and teacher both initiate events in their own way, whereas in the custodial-care approach (not represented in this study), child and teacher both respond to the flow of events, and the teacher's job is merely to keep the child safe and out of trouble. While this approach is common, it does not qualify as a candidate for use in programs meant to contribute to children's development.

The Direct Instruction curriculum model, developed by Carl Bereiter and Siegfried Engelmann (1966), represents the programmed-learning approach. The model began with a preschool program devoted to behavioral learning principles that Bereiter and Engelmann operated at the University of Illinois–Urbana in the mid-1960s. The model, which was eventually adapted to use in Follow Through primary-grade programs, also

Figure 1

FOUR THEORETICAL APPROACHES TO EARLY CHILDHOOD EDUCATION

	Child responds	*Child initiates*
Teacher initiates	Programmed-learning approach	Open-framework approach
Teacher responds	Custodial-care approach	Child-centered approach

became the basis of the *DISTAR* materials published by Science Research Associates. Direct Instruction focuses on academics — specifically, on the content of intelligence and achievement tests. In Direct Instruction, teachers lead small groups of children in precisely planned 20-minute question-and-answer lessons in language, mathematics, and reading. Workbooks are the only materials in the classroom. The developers have found that Direct Instruction suits elementary school teachers better than it suits preschool teachers. This may be because it is a model that seeks to perfect teacher-centered education (which is common in elementary schools), rather than to convert teachers to child-centered education (which is more common in preschool programs).

The Nursery School curriculum model, encompassing what has traditionally been seen as good early childhood education (Sears & Dowley, 1963), represents the child-centered approach. It is said to be "unit-based," because teachers center class activities, discussions, and field trips around broad units, or themes, such as community helpers, circus animals, or holidays. Within a permissive atmosphere, teachers expect children to show good manners, cooperate, and observe limits. Within a loose structure, children have freedom to choose activities, move from one activity to another, and interact with adults and peers. The emphasis is on developing social rather than intellectual skills.

The High/Scope curriculum model, developed by David P. Weikart and his associates (Hohmann, Banet, & Weikart, 1979; Hohmann & Weikart, 1995; Weikart, Rogers, Adcock, & McClelland, 1971), represents the open-framework approach. Based on Piaget's constructivist theory of child development, adults treat children as active learners and arrange their classrooms with discrete, well-equipped and labeled interest areas. Each day, children *plan, do,* and *review* the activities they carry out in these interest areas and engage actively in teacher-initiated small- and large-group activities. Teachers play a supportive rather than a directive role, facilitating children's intellectual, social, and physical *key experiences.* These key experiences represent the important domains of young children's development: initiative and social relations; creative representation; music; movement; language and literacy; classification; seriation; number; space; and time.

Documentation

Teaching staff in each program, together with the staff supervisor, wrote in a booklet an exact description of how they carried out their assigned model during the 1969–70 school year.

The booklet for the Direct Instruction model (originally called the Language Training Curriculum) began by describing home visits, then outlined the day, which included a reading group, a language group, and an arithmetic group (McClelland, Hiatt, Mainwaring, & Weathers, 1970). Language-group objectives, for example, included identity statements, plural statements, parts of the body, and categories. Teachers described their experiences in operating the program month by month. They addressed common questions about the program, noting that children had 15 minutes of free play daily; that they did *not* discipline children by placing them in dimly lit closets as was originally recommended by Bereiter and Engelmann (1966), and that the children were happy and busy. The booklet concludes with sample lessons.

The booklet for the High/Scope model (originally called the Cognitively Oriented Curriculum) presented the model's theoretical framework — which employs Piaget's stages of development, cognitive skill areas, and levels of representation and operation. This was followed by an annotated bibliography (McClelland, Smith, Kluge, Hudson, & Taylor, 1970). After discussing the importance of teacher commitment, it described the classroom's arrangement into activity areas and the daily routine. This routine included a time for plan-do-review, cleanup, snacktime, outdoor or indoor activity, and circle times. The booklet also explained the roles of science, music, and art. It then gave examples of learning activities (involving pet store animals, a live snake, and puppets) and a sample daily plan and evaluation.

The booklet for the Nursery School model (then called the Unit-Based Curriculum) presented the program's goals (such as developing children's task persistence and ability to use sentences in conversation); units (such as fall, Halloween, and facial features); and stories about individual children (McClelland, Martin, Malte, & Richardson, 1970). It noted that the program had a "very slim theoretical frame," which was basically the idea that teachers intuitively follow the children's lead and shape children's explorations into solid learning experiences.

Weikart et al. (1978) reported on the systematic observation of the three preschool programs, using the Pupil Record of School Experience (PROSE; Medley, Schluck, & Ames, 1968), which had the advantage of focusing on individual children rather than on the teacher. Each of the three programs was observed over a 4-week period in the spring of 1970, using 37 categories with a median inter-observer agreement of 79%. Observers using the PROSE found the significant differences that are indicated in Table 4 on the next page, which generally agree with expected curriculum model differences.

As Table 4 shows, Direct Instruction adults spent significantly more time engaged with children and attending to groups of children than did High/Scope or Nursery School adults. Compared with the High/Scope and Nursery School children, the Direct Instruction children spent significantly more time engaged in convergent teacher-defined activities, attending to adults, and experiencing direct teaching (telling, showing); they spent significantly less time engaged with one another, engaged with one another in moderate play, doing routine work, cooperating with one another, engaged in divergent child-defined activities, and engaged in fantasy and role-play activities.

High/Scope adults spent significantly more time attending to individual children than did the Direct Instruction or Nursery School adults. High/Scope teachers (as distinguished from teacher aides) spent significantly less time attending to children than did Direct Instruction or Nursery School teachers. High/Scope children spent significantly less time listening passively to adults than did Direct Instruction or Nursery School children. Nursery School teacher aides spent significantly less time attending to children than did the High/Scope or Direct Instruction teacher aides.

Table 4

OBSERVED SIGNIFICANT DIFFERENCES BETWEEN PRESCHOOL PROGRAMS

	Percentage of Time		
Differences	Direct Instruction	High\Scope	Nursery School
Direct Instruction vs. other models			
Adults and children engaged with each other	46%*	31%	37%
Adults attended to groups of children	29%*	9%	19%
Children engaged in convergent, teacher-defined activities	72%*	48%	56%
Children attended to adults	42%*	30%	35%
Children experienced direct teaching (telling, showing)	33%*	12%	23%
Children engaged with one another	5%*	12%	13%
Children engaged with one another in moderate play	5%*	12%	12%
Children did routine work	4%*	10%	9%
Children cooperated with one another	2%*	6%	6%
Children engaged in divergent, child-defined activities	2%*	16%	11%
Children engaged in fantasy and role-play activities	0%*	11%	10%
High/Scope vs. other models			
Adults (teachers and teacher aides) attended to individual children	6%	13%*	7%
Teachers (as distinguished from teacher aides) paid attention to children	36%	22%*	33%
Children listened passively to adults	18%	4%*	18%
Nursery School vs. other models			
Teacher aides attended to children	6%	9%	2%*

Note. Adapted from Weikart et al. (1978); observers used the Pupil Record of School Experience (PROSE; Medley et al., 1968). Group differences were tested for statistical significance by applying confidence intervals for multinominal proportions based on the degree of inter-observer agreement (see Weikart et al., 1978, for details). In each row, the starred value is significantly different from the other two values.

Weikart et al. (1978) statistically analyzed 492 home visit reports — 12 of them on each of 41 of the 68 children in the study — to examine program differences in the home visits' settings, maternal behavior, and curriculum implementation. Mothers participated in 80% of the scheduled High/Scope home visits, which emphasized the mother engaging her child in activities that fostered logical thinking. Mothers participated in 80% of the scheduled Direct Instruction home visits, which emphasized the mother teaching her child such academic skills as letter recognition and simple arithmetic and paid scant attention to socioemotional development. Mothers participated in only 50% of the scheduled Nursery School home visits, in which the child engaged in various activities and the emphasis was on socioemotional development.

Weikart et al. (1978) summarized the written comments of 12 early childhood experts who visited the project during 1968 and 1969 — Kuno Beller, Marion Blank, Courtney Cazden, Joseph Glick, Edmund Gordon, J. McVicker Hunt, Lawrence Kohlberg, James Miller, Todd Risley, Leonard Sealey, Irving Sigel, and Burton White. Without advance knowledge of either the common or the unique goals of the three programs, all the consultants commented on the uniformly high degree of staff enthusiasm and commitment. They noted the ways the various curriculums emphasized children's language development and persistence at activities. They were impressed with the potential importance of biweekly home visits. They considered the Direct Instruction program to be faithful to the Bereiter-Engelmann model in its high degree of structure, teacher-initiated activities, motivated involvement of the children, effective use of positive reinforcement, and lack of spontaneous social interaction. They saw the High/Scope teachers as highly involved in adapting Piagetian ideas to the children's developmental levels; several of them saw the plan-do-review part of the daily routine as a means of developing children's impulse control. They saw the Nursery School program as having the most frequent spontaneous interaction between adults and children and among the children themselves; most of them noticed the children's high degree of task persistence despite the lack of structure. Some consultants saw Nursery School teachers as passive and withdrawn from children's activities, whereas others considered the children in that program to be dependent on the teachers to structure their activities and direct their attention.

Because the teachers were observed to follow the curriculum models closely, it is reasonable to attribute differences in child outcomes to curriculum model differences rather than to idiosyncratic teacher differences. Readers who wish to see for themselves how faithfully the three programs were implemented can view a videotape called *This Is the Way We Go to School.* Originally made as a film while the programs were in progress, this video documenting the study's program implementation is available from High/Scope Press.

Instrumentation and Data Collection

The High/Scope Preschool Curriculum Comparison study collected data annually from ages 3 to 8 and at ages 10, 15, and 23.

Previous Tests and Measures

A variety of tests were used to assess children's intellectual and linguistic performance annually from ages 3 to 8 and at age 10. Researchers administered the Stanford-Binet Intelligence Scale (Terman & Merrill, 1960) at ages 3, 4, 5, 6, 7, and 8; the Peabody Picture Vocabulary Test (Dunn, 1965) at ages 3, 4, and 5; the Arthur Adaptation of the Leiter International Performance Scale (Arthur, 1952) at ages 3, 4, and 5; the Illinois Test of Psycholinguistic Abilities (Kirk, McCarthy, & Kirk, 1968) at ages 3, 4, 5, 6, and 7; and the Wechsler Intelligence Scale for Children (Wechsler, 1974) at age 10. A High/Scope staff member administered school achievement tests to the study participants in small groups — California Achievement Tests (Lower Primary Form W; Tiegs & Clark, 1963) at ages 7 and 8 and Metropolitan Achievement Tests (Elementary Form F; Durost, Bixler, Wrightstone, Prescott, & Balow, 1971) at age 10. The study's interviewer gave individual study participants the Adult APL Survey (American College Testing Program, 1976) to assess their literacy at ages 15 and 23.

Preschool teachers in the project rated children in their classes at the end of the preschool program, using the 25-item Pupil Observation Checklist and the 21-item Classroom Behavior Checklist, Version One (Weikart et al., 1978). Elementary-school teachers rated children at the end of first and second grades, using the 15-item Classroom Behavior Checklist, Version Two (Weikart et al., 1978). The age-15 interview, also used in the High/Scope Perry Preschool Project's age-19 assessment (Berrueta-Clement, Schweinhart, Barnett, Epstein, & Weikart, 1984), lasted about an hour and examined study participants' misconduct, family relations, activities, mental health, and school attitudes. It included scales representing misconduct (Bachman & Johnston, 1978), perceived locus of control (Bialer, 1961), self-esteem (Rosenberg, 1965), and attitudes toward teachers and learning (Arlin & Hill, 1976).

Age-23 Interview

The age-23 interview, also used in the High/Scope Perry Preschool Project age-27 assessment, lasted 1½ to 2 hours and examined the following characteristics of study participants:

- Literacy (APL Survey; American College Testing Program, 1976)
- Schooling completed and planned, secondary and postsecondary programs, parents' schooling and expectations, frequency of reading
- Health, use of health services, sick days in past year, smoking and drinking
- Employment status, history, and plans; job characteristics, satisfaction
- Marital status, spouse's schooling and employment, times married
- Income of respondent; spouse and others in household in past month and year; bank accounts; alimony and child support; years on welfare in past 10 years
- Living arrangements and household dwelling
- Reproductive history
- Rearing of oldest child, learning opportunities and practices, preschool program enrollment, child's schooling, respondent's support for schooling
- Getting along with others, family of origin; sources of irritation (Freeberg, 1976)

- Self-reported misconduct (Bachman & Johnston, 1978), school suspensions and expulsions, arrests, time in jail or on probation
- Car ownership, traffic tickets, wearing a seat belt
- Community activities, importance of religion, group memberships, voting, civic meetings or volunteer activities
- Ease in everyday activities
- Personal influences, 5-year goals, life's frustrations and positive aspects (open-ended questions)
- Interviewer ratings of the respondent's behavior during the interview

After the interview, the interviewer asked each respondent to sign consent forms for release of personal information from school, police, and social services records; each respondent was paid $50 for being interviewed.

Van Loggins — a long-time African-American resident well-known in Ypsilanti — found and interviewed study participants at ages 15 and 23. Because he had been a coach at Ypsilanti High School when the study participants were attending high school, he knew many of them and had at one time coached several of them. He was able to find many participants by obtaining information from their families and friends. He was not informed about which curriculum group individual study participants belonged to.

School and Arrest Records

Researchers collected data on 46 study participants from the general and special education records of the Ypsilanti Public School District and other school districts in Washtenaw County. Study participants had given their permission in advance for these records searches.

The full sample of 68 cases was included in our analysis of arrest records. Unlike missing school records, which simply count as missing data, missing arrest records signify the absence of arrests, giving a particular study participant a score of 0 for *number of arrests.* Although 87% of the total sample interviewed at age 23 still lived in Michigan (with 75% of the age-23 group still in Washtenaw County), as an added safeguard, geographic stability was taken into account in our analysis of felony arrests.

Arrest records came from summer and fall 1990 searches for study participants' paper records in Washtenaw County Juvenile Court; Washtenaw County Circuit Court; Washtenaw County District Court 14A, 14B, and 15; Detroit Recorder Court; Federal Court in Detroit; and computer records in the Michigan State Police Law Enforcement Information System.[6] These data have natural limitations. In particular, Michigan's state police system has only the information that local police and courts provide — which is relatively complete regarding arrests but less so regarding charges and even

[6]Despite repeated requests, the Federal Bureau of Investigation did not provide arrest data from its national record system.

less so regarding adjudications. Study participants who had been interviewed had given their permission in advance for these records searches; adult arrest records, however, are public information that is available for public inspection without the permission of those arrested.

Data Analysis Techniques

Curriculum group analyses were carried out without making statistical adjustments by blocking or using covariates, because the experimental design warranted it and because sample sizes of 46 to 68 cases are not large enough to support such fine-grained analyses. For example, carrying out a three-way analysis of variance using curriculum group by gender by race (3 x 2 x 2) on the full sample results in 12 cells with 2 to 11 members each, including 5 cells with 5 or fewer members; the statistics of an outcome variable for cells with so few members are undependable.

For *categorical variables,* the study compares the percentages of curriculum group members in the various categories and presents the two-tailed probability of the differences, using the chi-square statistic. When the three groups were found to be significantly different with a probability of less than .05, pairs of groups were then compared using the same procedure. For *continuous variables,* the study compares the means of the curriculum groups and presents the two-tailed probability of the differences, using analysis of variance. When the three groups were found to be significantly different with a probability of less than .05, we used Bonferroni post-hoc analysis to compare pairs of groups (this corrects for multiple comparisons by dividing the observed significance level of the *t* test of a comparison by the number of comparisons made).

Because many variables had unusual distributions and unequal group variances, continuous variables were also analyzed using the Kruskal-Wallis statistic corrected for ties, a nonparametric procedure that uses the chi-square statistic to test differences in the mean ranks of groups. Mean ranks are calculated by ranking all the scores in the sample, then averaging the ranks achieved by each curriculum group. However, examination of the findings revealed that analysis of variance and the Kruskal-Wallis statistic seldom differed in their conclusions regarding whether curriculum group differences were statistically significant for the variable in question. So we present the mean ranks and Kruskal-Wallis analysis only for those few variables where discrepant findings were obtained. When the three curriculum groups were found to be significantly different with a probability of less than .05, pairs of groups were then compared using the same procedure.

Because meaningful differences can fail to achieve the conventional .05 level of statistical significance in small samples, the tables present exact two-tailed *p*-values up to .10. There is nothing magical about the conventionally designated .05 level of significance, and we believe that readers deserve to know which findings have at least a 90% probability of not being chance occurrences. However, in this report, we consider and treat a finding as statistically significant only when the conventional .05

level of statistical significance has been achieved; in the tables, therefore, any *p*-values at the .05 level or less are emphasized by boldface type.

Data analyses were conducted using SPSS for Windows, Version 6.1 (Norušis, 1993).

Methodological Criticisms and Responses

Once the High/Scope Preschool Curriculum Comparison Study's age-15 results were made public, Bereiter (1986) and Gersten (1986) suggested that the study's interviewer knew which preschool curriculum model the 15-year-olds had experienced (the interviewer had no knowledge of which curriculum groups respondents belonged to); that Weikart influenced elementary and secondary school staff's treatment of study participants in their post-preschool years (Weikart left the employment of the Ypsilanti Public School District in 1970 to establish the High/Scope Educational Research Foundation); that the sample size was too small to provide confidence in the results (assurance of confidence-level is the purpose of tests of statistical significance); and that results were not reported using the conventional .05 level of statistical significance (they were, but levels between .05 and .10 were also reported as an aid to interpretation, as is the case in this report as well). They also questioned the validity of self-report measures of delinquency (widely used by delinquency researchers) and the comparability of the curriculum groups in background characteristics (at program entry, groups differed significantly on only one variable, mothers' highest year of schooling; the fact that the Nursery School group was significantly better-off than the High/Scope group on this variable was taken into account in additional analyses).

Bereiter (1986), after suggesting that the High/Scope group be removed from the analysis (a suggestion inconsistent with the purpose of the study), then questioned the significance of the misconduct difference between the remaining Direct Instruction and Nursery School groups (the exact *p*-level of the difference was .055). Bereiter (1986) and Gersten (1986) further suggested that the findings were sensationalized and blown out of proportion by the media (all the news reports of the findings were accurate) and asked how Direct Instruction could improve school success and not reduce delinquency (a question that assumes that school success always prevents delinquency).

In presenting the design of this study, this chapter has made a strong case for the study's internal validity — its ability to provide a meaningful answer to the research question of whether and how well-implemented preschool curriculum models significantly differ in their effects, short- and long-term, on young people born into poverty. The next chapter presents the differences in effects through age 23 of study participants.

III Differences in Curriculum Groups Through Age 23

The internal validity of the High/Scope Preschool Curriculum Comparison Study provides strong assurances that differences between the outcomes of the curriculum groups is due to differences between the preschool programs they experienced. This chapter presents findings for curriculum-group differences through age 23 in the following domains:

- Schooling (test scores, educational activities, planned future schooling, school records)
- Household and family (participants' living arrangements, participants' childrearing)
- Employment and income (employment history, earnings, welfare assistance)
- Personal and community activities (voting, sources of irritation, interviewer ratings, 5-year plans, positive and negative aspects of life)
- Misconduct and crime (self-reported misconduct, official records of felony arrests, types of crimes)

Schooling

Test Scores

No differences in the average test scores of curriculum groups appeared consistently over time, on either the Stanford-Binet Intelligence Test given annually from ages 3 to 7 (Terman & Merrill, 1960), the Peabody Picture Vocabulary Test given at ages 4 and 5 (Dunn, 1965), the Arthur Adaptation of the Leiter International Performance Scale given at ages 4 and 5 (Arthur, 1952), the Illinois Test of Psycholinguistic Abilities given annually from ages 4 to 7 (Kirk, McCarthy, & Kirk, 1968), the Wechsler Intelligence Scale for Children given at age 10 (Wechsler, 1974), the California Achievement Tests given at ages 7 and 8 (Tiegs & Clark, 1963), the Metropolitan Achievement Tests given at age 10 (Durost et al., 1971), or the Adult APL Survey given at ages 15 and 23 (American College Testing Program, 1976). Table 5 on the next page lists only one significant difference: The Direct Instruction group surpassed the Nursery School group at the end of the preschool program (age 5) on the Stanford-Binet Intelligence Scale.

Significant curriculum group differences also appeared from time to time on mean subtest scores but never at consecutive testings. (The tables do not present subtest scores.) Out of 20 comparisons on the Illinois Test of Psycholinguistic Abilities, 4 yielded significant differences, but none of these differences were consistent across two consecutive years. In all of them, the Direct Instruction group scored significantly higher than the Nursery School group, echoing the findings on the Stanford-Binet Intelligence Scale at the end of the preschool program at age 5. The differences were on the following subtests:

Table 5

GROUP COMPARISONS OF TEST PERFORMANCE OVER TIME

Variable	All Programs	Direct Instruction	High/ Scope	Nursery School	p
Intellectual performance (IQ) at study entry (Stanford-Binet)	78.3 (6.8)	78.8 (7.0)	77.5 (7.0)	78.6 (6.8)	—
Intellectuaal performance (IQ) after the first of two preschool years (Stanford-Binet; $n = 50$)	105.2 (12.5)	107.5 (13.7)	105.8 (14.6)	102.1 (7.4)	—
Intellectual performance (IQ) at age 5, the end of preschool program (Stanford-Binet)	97.5 (11.2)	103.2* (11.9)	96.5 (11.9)	92.7* (7.0)	**.005**
Intellectual performance (IQ) at age 6 (Stanford-Binet, $n = 61$)	95.3 (12.1)	98.1 (13.6)	94.9 (13.0)	92.2 (8.5)	—
Intellectual performance (IQ) at age 7 (Stanford-Binet, $n = 64$)	95.3 (11.8)	96.7 (12.5)	93.7 (13.5)	95.6 (9.6)	—
Intellectual performance (IQ) at age 10 (Wechsler Intelligence Scale for Children, $n = 35$)	95.2 (14.1)	97.4 (13.8)	96.2 (16.0)	91.5 (13.1)	—
School achievement at age 7 (California Achievement Test raw score; $n = 64$)	102.6 (42.5)	99.6 (41.7)	102.1 (46.8)	105.9 (40.9)	—
School achievement at age 8 (California Achievement Test raw score; $n = 65$)	160.6 (45.2)	160.0 (49.4)	167.0 (47.0)	154.3 (38.9)	—
School achievement at age 10 (Metropolitan Achievement Test raw score; $n = 27$)	134.7 (52.0)	133.6 (59.4)	121.7 (33.9)	158.2 (62.8)	—
Literacy at age 15 (APL Survey, possible score = 40, $n = 52$, $r_{\alpha} = 856$)	18.0 (6.2)	16.9 (5.6)	18.7 (7.5)	18.4 (5.4)	—
Literacy at 23[a] (APL Survey, possible score = 40, $n = 47$, $r_{\alpha} = .878$)	24.0 (7.4)	23.2 (7.8)	23.6 (7.9)	25.1 (7.0)	—

Note. $n = 68$ unless otherwise indicated. Because they are based on three cohorts, the values presented here differ from those presented in previous reports based on two cohorts. The analysis of variance tests differences in means (followed by standard deviations in parentheses). One curriculum group value in a row is starred if different from the other two curriculum group's values at $p < .05$; two group values in a row are starred if different from each other at $p < .05$.

[a]The Pearson correlation coefficient between literacy at age 15 and at age 23 was .521 ($n = 36$, $p = .001$).

- At the end of the preschool program, *Auditory Association* (verbal analogies, such as "I cut with a saw; I pound with a _____.")
- At the end of the first preschool program year and at the end of kindergarten, *Verbal Expression* (verbally describing familiar objects, such as a ball)
- At the end of the first preschool program year, *Auditory Reception* (showing understanding of verbal materials, such as "Do dials yawn?")

Also, at age 15 but not at age 23, the Direct Instruction group had a significantly lower average score than the other curriculum groups on the Occupational Knowledge subscale of the APL Survey.

The more important finding from tests is the extraordinary increase in the mean IQ of the whole sample of children, whatever curriculum model they experienced. From the age-3 baseline mean IQ of 78, the three curriculum groups together at age 4 evidenced an average improvement of 26 points after 1 year of the preschool programs. This improvement diminished by 9 points over the subsequent 2 years, but then held relatively steady through age 10, when it was 17 points above the baseline. This pattern of findings distinguishes this study as one of the few reporting sustained improvement in intellectual performance through age 10, providing counter-evidence to the notion that there is a complete fade-out of preschool's effects on IQ.

Teacher Ratings

Using the Classroom Behavior Checklist, Version Two (Weikart et al., 1978), teachers did not rate curriculum groups significantly differently on sociability or cooperation at first or second grade or on independence at first grade. They did, however, rate the Nursery School group as significantly more independent ($p = .037$, $n = 27$) at second grade (mean = 4.9, $SD = 1.7$) than the Direct Instruction group (mean = 3.0, $SD = 1.7$); the High/Scope group was in the middle (mean = 4.4, $SD = 0.9$). The High/Scope group was rated as nonsignificantly more cooperative ($p = .127$) at first grade (mean = 5.0, $SD = 1.7$) than the Direct Instruction group (mean = 3.3, $SD = 1.6$).

Educational Activities

As Table 6 (on p. 38) shows, the age-15 finding that significantly more members of the Nursery School group than of the Direct Instruction group held a school office or job was not repeated in the age-23 findings. As might be expected, sample members' later recollections of such minor high school occurrences apparently bore little resemblance to their reporting of them several years earlier, when they were high school age.

As Table 6 also shows, the three curriculum groups did not differ significantly in grade-point average, highest year of schooling, on-time high school graduation rate, high school graduation/GED rate, or patterns of post-high-school education. However, both *grade-point average* and *on-time high school graduation rate* were lowest for the Direct Instruction group, higher for the High/Scope group, and highest for the Nursery School group. The 47% on-time high school graduation rate of the Direct Instruction group was 17 percentage points lower than the High/Scope group's 64% and 25 percentage points lower than the Nursery School group's 72%. This pattern is strikingly similar to the findings of the Karnes study, in which the high school graduation rate was 48% for the Direct Instruction group, as compared with 70% for the traditional Nursery

Table 6

GROUP COMPARISONS OF SELF-REPORTED SCHOOLING

Variable	Direct Instruction	High/ Scope	Nursery School	p
Elected/appointed to school office or job, reported at age 15 (*n* = 53)	0%*	12%	33%*	**.018**
Elected/appointed to school office or job, reported at age 23	16%	7%	16%	—
Grade-point average (*n* = 40, possible = 4.00)	1.36 (1.10)	1.60 (0.87)	1.87 (1.16)	—
Highest year of schooling[a] (*n* = 51)	12.1 (2.0)	12.4 (1.7)	12.7 (1.7)	—
4-year college degree	5%	0%	0%	
2 or more years of college	21%	21%	33%	
Up to 1 year of college	5%	21%	11%	
Vocational school	0%	0%	6%	
High school graduate	16%	21%	22%	
Some high school	42%	29%	22%	
On-time high school graduation (*n* = 51)	47%	64%	72%	—
High school graduation/GED (*n* = 51)	58%	71%	78%	—
Any post-high-school education/training (*n* = 50)	61%	77%	79%	—
Current program (*n* = 50)				
4-year college	5%	7%	11%	—
2-year college	5%	21%	6%	
Vocational/technical/apprenticeship	11%	0%	6%	
High school/continuing education	0%	7%	0%	
Highest year of schooling planned[a] (*n* = 44)	14.1* (2.2)	16.3* (1.8)	15.1 (2.2)	**.020**
Doctoral degree	0%	8%	0%	
Master's degree	12%	23%	21%	
Bachelor's degree	24%	39%	36%	
2 or more years of college	18%	31%	14%	
Vocational certification	12%	0%	14%	
High school equivalent	35%	0%	14%	

Note. $n = 52$ unless otherwise indicated. The chi-square statistic tests differences in percentages; the analysis of variance tests differences in means (followed by standard deviations in parentheses). The associated p-value is reported if less than .100. One group value in a row is starred if different from the other two at $p < .05$; two group values in a row are starred if different from each other at $p < .05$.

[a]Junior high school = 9, some high school = 10.5, high school graduate or GED = 12, vocational training or community college = 12.5, 1 year of college = 13, 2-year college degree = 14, 2 or more years of college = 15, 4-year college degree = 16, master's degree = 18, doctoral degree = 20.

School group; the Karnes study did not have an analogue to the High/Scope group (Karnes et al., 1983). The pattern also resembles the High/Scope Perry Preschool Project's finding that 66% of the program group but only 45% of the no-program group graduated from high school on time. The two studies — the High/Scope Preschool Curriculum Comparison Study and the High/Scope Perry Preschool Project — in fact found parallel inter-group patterns for several key outcome variables.

Planned Schooling

Members of the High/Scope group planned to go to school significantly longer (2.2 years longer) than did members of the Direct Instruction group. On average, the High/Scope group saw themselves as completing 4 years of college, while the Direct Instruction group anticipated completing 2 years of college. Every member of the High/Scope group planned to complete at least 2 years of college, while only 54% of the Direct Instruction group planned to complete at least 2 years of college. These results express educational aspirations; they may later become differences in educational attainment or perhaps differences in other aspects of socioeconomic success and responsibility.

School Records

Table 7 (on p. 40) presents information from school records. The High/Scope group experienced significantly more years of compensatory education than did the Nursery School group,[7] which experienced no compensatory education. (Assignment to compensatory education is based on family income and school achievement.) It is interesting to compare this finding with the High/Scope Perry Preschool Project finding that the program group, who experienced the High/Scope Curriculum, underwent more years of compensatory education than did the no-program group. In that study, the program versus no-program difference in years of compensatory education was more than offset by an opposite difference in the two groups' years of special education for educable mental impairment, whereas in this study it was more than offset by an opposite difference in the two groups' years of special education for emotional impairment.

The Direct Instruction group experienced significantly more years of special education for emotional impairment or disturbance — averaging over 1 year per member — than did either of the other two groups — whose members averaged almost no time in such education. Nearly half (47%) of those in the Direct Instruction group, compared with only 6% in either of

---

[7]Although the Bonferroni post-hoc analysis did not identify this pairwise comparison as significant, these were the extremes of the three-way comparison (see footnote 11, p. 59). This difference was partly due to the group difference in mother's highest year of schooling; when this variable was used as a covariate, the significance level of the group comparison dropped to .100.

Table 7

GROUP COMPARISONS OF SCHOOL RECORDS

Variable	Direct Instruction	High/Scope	Nursery School	p
Years of general education	10.9 (1.0)	11.5 (1.7)	11.4 (1.4)	—
Years of compensatory education	0.3 (0.6)	0.6* (1.0)	0.0* (0.0)	**.049**
% spending 1–3 years	20%	33%	0%	
Overall years of special education[a]	1.9 (1.6)	2.1 (3.1)	1.7 (2.7)	—
Years of special education for identified disability:	1.8 (2.0)	1.9 (3.8)	1.7 (2.7)	—
% spending 1–2 years	47%	20%	13%	
% spending 3–10 years	33%	33%	31%	
Years of identified educable mental impairment (EMI)	0.2 (0.6)	1.1 (2.9)	0.8 (2.3)	—
% ever identified as EMI	13%	13%	13%	
Years of identified emotional impairment or disturbance (EI)	1.1* (1.5)	0.1 (0.5)	0.1 (0.3)	**.004**
% ever identified as EI	47%	6%	6%	
Years of identified specific learning disability (LD)	0.3 (0.9)	0.6 (1.7)	0.4 (1.0)	—
% ever identified as LD	13%	13%	13%	
Years of identified speech-and-language impairment (SLI)	0.1 (0.4)	0.1 (0.4)	0.4 (1.0)	—
% ever identified as SLI	13%	13%	19%	
Years repeating a grade	0.3 (0.6)	0.5 (0.7)	0.3 (0.6)	—
% ever repeated a grade	20%	40%	19%	
Years in correctional/disciplinary program	0.0 (0.0)	0.1 (0.3)	0.1 (0.5)	—
Total number of subjects failed	9.6 (7.0)	5.0 (5.5)	4.9 (4.9)	.053
Days absent per school year	6.4 (4.2)	8.3 (4.5)	6.7 (7.0)	—
Total times dropped out of school	0.13 (0.34)	0.32 (0.72)	0.13 (0.34)	—
Times dropped out and returned	0.00 (0.00)	0.14 (0.35)	0.00 (0.00)	**.037**

Note. $n = 46$ unless otherwise indicated. The analysis of variance tests differences in means (followed by standard deviations in parentheses). The p-value is reported if less than .100. One group value in a row is starred if different from the other two at $p < .05$; two group values in a row are starred if different from each other at $p < .05$.

[a]*Special education* combines self-contained classes, integrated classes, and speech-and-language support.

the other curriculum groups, were at some time identified as having emotional impairment or disturbance. As a consequence, although not a significant difference, 80% of the Direct Instruction group spent some time in special education, as compared with only 53% of the High/Scope group and 44% of the Nursery School group.

Direct Instruction group members failed in almost twice as many subjects as did the members of the other two curriculum groups — a difference that was nearly significant and that was also consistent with the nonsignificant pattern of the Direct Instruction group having a lower grade-point average and a lower on-time high school graduation rate than the other two curriculum groups.

The three curriculum groups did not differ significantly in the average number of times their members dropped out of school. However, compared with the other two groups, High/Scope group members were significantly more likely to return to high school after dropping out (Direct Instruction and Nursery School group members never returned to high school after dropping out.) No significant curriculum group differences were found for years of general education; overall years of special education; years of special education for educable mental impairment, specific learning disability, or speech-and-language impairment; years retained in grade; years in a correctional or disciplinary program; days absent per school year; or total times dropped out of school.

Household and Family

Age 23, which is at the very beginning of adult life, is still very much a transitional period. The striking evidence of this is that, as shown in Table 8 (on p. 42), nearly half the respondents in each curriculum group (47% overall) were living with their mother and/or father.

Living Arrangements

As shown in Table 8, the High/Scope and Direct Instruction groups differed significantly in the percentages *living with spouse;* 31% of the High/Scope group, as compared with 0% of the Direct Instruction group, were living with their spouse. As might be expected, when asked their *marital status,* similar percentages of these respective groups reported being *married;* however, slight differences in sample size kept the *married* percentages from being significantly different across curriculum groups (as the *living with spouse* percentages were). These findings resemble the High/Scope Perry Preschool Project finding that 40% of program females but only 8% of no-program females were married at age 27 ($n = 49$, $p = .036$).

Curriculum groups did not differ significantly in *number of persons per household at age 23, past and present pregnancies of females, number of children per member,* or *times moved to a new residence.* However, com-

Table 8

GROUP COMPARISONS OF HOUSEHOLD AND FAMILY CHARACTERISTICS AT AGE 23

Characteristic	Direct Instruction	High/ Scope	Nursery School	*p*
Persons living in respondent's household (n = 49)				
Mother &/or father	53%	46%	41%	—
Other relatives	10%	0%	12%	—
Spouse[a]	0%*	31%*	18%	**.045**
Cohabitant	21%	15%	18%	—
Roommate	16%	8%	0%	—
Alone	5%	0%	6%	—
Marital status				
Married	0%	29%	16%	—
Cohabiting	21%	7%	11%	
Divorced or separated	11%	0%	5%	
Single, never married	68%	64%	68%	
Number of persons in household	4.7 (2.6)	3.8 (1.8)	3.5 (2.6)	—
Past and present pregnancies of females[b] (n = 27)	1.8 (1.6)	0.8 (0.9)	1.2 (1.7)	—
0	33%	50%	50%	
1–2	22%	50%	33%	
3–5	44%	0%	20%	
Per-member number of children (n = 48)	1.2 (1.2)	0.5 (0.9)	0.6 (0.9)	—
0	39%	67%	67%	
1	22%	25%	17%	
2–3	39%	8%	17%	
Times moved to a new residence	3.4 (3.7)	2.8 (2.2)	2.4 (2.1)	—
How family feels about how you are doing at age 15 (n = 54)	1.7* (0.5)	2.1 (0.2)	2.0 (0.3)	**.005**
Doing great (3)	0%	6%	6%	
Getting by okay (2)	67%	94%	89%	
Not doing anything worth much (1)	33%	0%	6%	
How family feels about how you are doing at age 23	2.0 (0.7)	2.5 (0.5)	2.4 (0.7)	.054
Doing great (3)	21%	50%	53%	
Getting by okay (2)	58%	50%	37%	
Not doing anything worth much (1)	21%	0%	11%	

Note. n = 52 unless otherwise indicated. The chi-square statistic tests differences in percentages; the analysis of variance tests differences in means (followed by standard deviations in parentheses). The associated p-value is reported if less than .100. One group value in a row is starred if different from the other two at $p < .05$. Two group values in a row are starred if different from each other at $p < .05$.

[a]Percentages for *spouse living in household* and *married* differ because of different sample sizes.

[b]Three women were pregnant at the time of the interview. Of 16 women responding, one had one abortion, one had two abortions, and three had one miscarriage each.

pared with the Direct Instruction females, the High/Scope females reported experiencing fewer than half as many pregnancies (0.8 vs. 1.8) and having fewer than half as many children (0.5 vs. 1.2). These findings resemble the High/Scope Perry Preschool Project finding that program females, by age 19, had experienced half as many pregnancies as no-program females (0.6 vs. 1.2, $n = 49$, $p = .084$).

One significant difference at age 15, as Table 8 shows, was that only two thirds of the Direct Instruction group reported that their families felt they were *doing great* or *getting by okay;* this compared with all of the High/Scope group and 95% of the Nursery School group. A similar pattern appeared at age 23 with a significance level of .054. At age 23, only 21% of the Direct Instruction group members reported that their families felt that they were *doing great;* this compared with 50% of the High/Scope group and 53% of the Nursery School group. At age 15, the finding about family opinion was consistent with the Direct Instruction group's larger number of acts of misconduct. As will be seen, a similar consistency is in evidence at age 23.

Participants' Childrearing

In an attempt to see if the programs differed in their effects on the children of the participants, the interviewer asked study participants to identify a child whom they had a major role in raising; 44% of them did so, 21 respondents in all — with 11 in the Direct Instruction group, 4 in the High/Scope group, and 6 in the Nursery School group. Of these 21 respondents, 86% identified a son or daughter, and 14% identified some other young relative; 57% of the identified children were 1 to 5 years old, and 43% were 6 to 11 years old; 48% of the children were female, and 52% were male. The three curriculum groups did not differ on these measures, on a scale of educational materials provided for the child, or on a scale of educational activities engaged in by the child.

From a list of 10 types of *educational materials,* 21 sample members reported providing their child with an average of 5.9 types ($SD = 2.3$; $n = 21$). The percentages making available each type of material are as follows: paper and writing materials (86%), age-appropriate children's books (81%), other drawing materials (76%), children's records or cassettes (76%), craft materials (62%), computer (62%), musical instruments (52%), dictionary (57%), encyclopedia (33%), and blocks or other educational toys (5%). Most surprising is the 62% reporting availability of computers as contrasted with the 5% reporting availability of blocks or other educational toys.

When asked to indicate the frequency of certain *educational activities* for the child (1 = never, 2 = once in a while, 3 = sometimes, 4 = frequently), the 21 sample members' average ranking was 3.3 ($SD = 0.5$). The educational activities (with the sample's mean ranking for each item in parentheses) are these: eat together (3.9); teach simple learning skills, such as counting, writing one's name, reciting the alphabet (3.8); have peers over to play (3.7); teach active skills, such as riding a bike, cooking, sports (3.5); read books to child (3.2); discuss television programs (3.1); and go to museums/libraries (1.5).

Economic Status

Employment and Income

Because 23-year-olds are only at the beginning of their work careers, their current employment and earnings are not good predictors of their lifetime work or career patterns. (Highest year of schooling is the lifetime earnings predictor variable preferred by economists.) Still in a period of transition, 23-year-olds are trying out possibilities, so their work patterns may be somewhat erratic. To illustrate, the age-23 mean annual income in this study was $6,289, whereas it was $12,210 — almost twice as much — for the 27-year-olds in the High/Scope Perry Preschool Project. Nevertheless, it is interesting to examine Table 9 data to see if preliminary economic trends emerge for the High/Scope Preschool Curriculum Comparison Study participants at age 23.

We can see mixed evidence that the High/Scope group had a lower employment rate and lower reported earnings than the Nursery School group, with employment and earnings of the Direct Instruction group falling somewhere in between. Table 9 shows one statistically significant difference supporting this conclusion: *Past year's earnings from work* averaged $8,881 for the Nursery School group versus $3,738 for the High/Scope group (with the Direct Instruction group averaging $5,769). This finding is echoed by the nearly significant difference in *past year's household income from all sources,* which averaged $9,798 for the Nursery School group versus $4,391 for the High/Scope group (with the Direct Instruction group averaging $6,442). On both of these variables, the High/Scope group's figure was about half the size of the Nursery School group's figure. The patterns on three additional variables, though they do not involve significant differences, also suggest the Nursery School group's economic superiority over the High/Scope group:

- *Monthly earnings from work* averaged $698 for the Nursery School group, but only $465 for the High/Scope group (with the Direct Instruction group in between, with a $498 average).
- *Current employment* rates were 72% for the Nursery School group versus 50% for the High/Scope group (with the Direct Instruction group highest of all, with a 79% rate).
- Number of *months in the last 24 neither employed nor in school* averaged 3.1 months for the Nursery School group versus 5.3 months for the High/Scope group. (The finding on this variable for the Direct Instruction group — 7.7 months neither employed nor in school — was the highest of the three groups and thus contradicted the finding that the Direct Instruction group had the highest current employment rate.)

A nonsignificant difference on one variable, however, casts doubt on any conclusion about the economic superiority of the Nursery School group: Respondent's average *monthly income from all sources* was highest for the High/Scope group — $1,378, as compared with $1,170 for the Nursery School group (and $730 for the Direct Instruction group).

Table 9

GROUP COMPARISONS OF ECONOMIC STATUS

Variable	Direct Instruction	High/ Scope	Nursery School	p
Ever employed during last 5 years	100%	100%	94%	—
Months in last 24 neither employed nor in school (n = 48)	7.7 (8.2)	5.3 (8.4)	3.1 (6.3)	—
0	33%	31%	65%	
1–6	17%	54%	24%	
7–24	39%	15%	12%	
Currently employed	79%	50%	72%	—
Monthly income of respondent				
Earnings from work (n = 48)	$498 ($324)	$465 ($445)	$698 ($477)	—
$0	12%	31%	11%	
$100–$500	35%	31%	33%	
$501–$1,600	53%	39%	55%	
Respondent's income from all sources (n = 38)	$730 ($691)	$1,378 ($1,005)	$1,170 ($876)	—
$0	7%	0%	0%	
$100–$1,000	71%	44%	60%	
$1,001–$3,500	21%	56%	40%	
Past year's income of respondent[a]				
Earnings from work (n = 45)	$5,769 ($4,523)	$3,738* ($4,636)	$8,881* ($6,516)	**.042**
Household income from all sources (n = 35)	$6,442 ($4,958)	$4,391 ($4,895)	$9,798 ($6,783)	.081
Months on welfare in last 10 years (n = 52)	13.3 (24.3)	9.3 (11.6)	13.7 (29.6)	—
0	63%	43%	58%	
1–12	16%	36%	21%	
13–108	21%	21%	21%	
Banking				
Savings or investments	58%	62%	61%	
Checking account (n = 50)	11%*	46%*	17%	**.046**
Own one or more cars	63%	50%	53%	—
Recent (vs. older) car (n = 28)	8%*	57%	78%	**.004**

Note. n = 52 unless otherwise indicated. The chi-square statistic tests differences in percentages; the analysis of variance tests differences in means (followed by standard deviations in parentheses). The associated p-value is reported if less than .100. One group value in a row is starred if different from the other two at $p < .05$; two group values in a row are starred if different from each other at $p < .05$.

[a]The statistical significance of group differences in *past year's income of respondent* was .067 when *mother's highest year of schooling* was used as a covariate.

To sum up, the evidence that the Nursery School group had an economic advantage over the High/Scope group is weak in that only one employment/income variable achieved a statistically significant difference, and the nonsignificant patterns just discussed went in both directions. Adding this to the fact that age-23 employment and income patterns are poor lifetime predictors, we conclude that it would be rash, at this time in this study, to draw any conclusions about preschool curriculum effects on employment and income.

Gender was found to play a weak role in employment status and earnings. In two-way analyses of variance, neither gender nor the gender-by-group interaction factor was statistically significant (or nearly so) for current employment status, respondent's monthly earnings, or respondent's annual earnings. However, the considerable size of the whole-group difference in annual earnings (the Nursery School versus High/Scope difference) was largely due to the 9 Nursery School females' average annual earnings of $9,189 as compared with the 8 High/Scope females' average annual earnings of only $2,325. Males' earnings were more similar across the two groups — the 7 Nursery School males reported earning an average of $8,486, while the 5 High/Scope males reported earning $6,000 annually.

With respect to current jobs, the curriculum groups did not differ in the hours worked per week, hourly wage, or satisfaction with various job aspects. Across the three groups, those currently employed worked an average of 36.3 hours a week (SD = 11.5, n = 33) and earned $5.77 per hour ($SD$ = $2.24, n = 29). Using a 4-point satisfaction scale (where 1 = very dissatisfied, 2 = fairly dissatisfied, 3 = fairly satisfied, and 4 = very satisfied, and r_α = .494), the respondents rated their attitudes toward their current job, pay, kind of work, coworkers, supervisor, and opportunity to advance; the average rating across the three groups was 3.1 (SD = 0.5, n = 29).

Welfare Assistance

Table 9 also shows that no curriculum group differences were found for *months on welfare in last 10 years,* that is, from ages 14 to 23. Averaging for the sample as a whole, we find that during those 10 years, 56% did not receive welfare assistance, 23% received welfare assistance for up to 1 year, 15% received welfare assistance for 1 to 5 years, and 6% received welfare assistance for 5 to 10 years. The three curriculum groups did not differ significantly in the percentages that received the various types of welfare assistance. Across the groups (52 interviewed sample members), 12% received Aid to Families with Dependent Children, 12% received food stamps, 12% received Medicaid, 8% received child support, and 2% received Supplemental Security Income. Neither did curriculum groups differ significantly in percentages receiving child support; 8% of all sample members received child support.

As Table 9 indicates, the curriculum groups did not differ significantly in the percentages having savings or investments, but nearly half of High/Scope group members had a checking account, while fewer than a fifth of the members of each of the other curriculum groups had a checking account. Although the curriculum groups did not differ significantly in their rate of car ownership (56% of the entire sample owned one or more cars), only one of the car owners in the Direct Instruction group reported having a "recent model," whereas about two thirds of the car owners in the other two curriculum groups reported having a recent model.

Personal and Community Activities

Voting

The three curriculum groups differed significantly on various personal and community activities, as shown in Table 10 (on p. 48). Compared with the Direct Instruction group, significantly higher percentages of the High/Scope and Nursery School groups had *ever done volunteer work;* also, more High/Scope and Nursery School group members had *registered to vote,* but group differences for this variable were not significant. A significantly greater percentage of the High/Scope group than of the Direct Instruction or Nursery School groups had *voted in the last Presidential election,* about three times as many. Of the three groups, the Nursery School group reported the greatest percentage having *voted in the last state or local election,* but the differences on this variable were not significant.

Other Activities

Across the three curriculum groups, similar percentages reported that they *belong to one or two community groups;* 23% of the entire sample answered yes to this question. At age 15, significantly more members of the High/Scope group than of the Direct Instruction group reported playing ball or other sports — 94% versus 45%; however, this question was not repeated on the age-23 interview. The curriculum groups did not differ in their perceived *ease of doing things,* as measured by a 12-item scale indicating how easy a respondent found it to learn new skills, keep a job or stay in school, feel close to family and friends, and so on. To a nearly significant extent, the curriculum groups differed in the percentages who said they drink alcoholic beverages: While 26% of the Direct Instruction and 28% of the Nursery School groups reported drinking *several times a week or daily,* none of the High/Scope group reported drinking with this frequency.

Sources of Irritation

As shown in Table 10 and Figure 2, the Direct Instruction group identified significantly more sources of irritation than the High/Scope group did (the interview item asked respondents to identify "different types of people . . .

Table 10

GROUP COMPARISONS OF PERSONAL AND COMMUNITY ACTIVITIES

Variable	Direct Instruction	High/ Scope	Nursery School	p
Ever done volunteer work	11%*	43%	44%	**.047**
Registered to vote	37%	62%	56%	—
Voted in last presidential election	21%	62%*	22%	**.030**
Voted in state or local election	5%	8%	29%	.086
Belong to one or two community groups[a]	26%	28%	16%	—
Play ball, other sports at age 15 (n = 54)	1.6* (0.2)	2.4* (0.6)	2.2 (0.9)	**.006**
A lot	17%	50%	44%	
Sometimes	28%	44%	28%	
Never, hardly ever	56%	6%	28%	
Ease of doing things[b] (mean rating on 12 items; r_α = .862)	3.2 (0.6)	3.2 (0.5)	3.2 (0.5)	—
Drink alcoholic beverages (n = 51)				
Never or once in a while	74%	100%	72%	.094
Several times a week or daily	26%	0%	28%	
Sources of irritation (mean count on 12 items; r_α = .594)	2.0* (2.0)	0.4* (0.6)	1.2 (1.2)	**.014**
Law (r_α = .527)	0.6 (0.9)	0.1 (0.4)	0.2 (0.5)	.068
Police	32%	14%	5%	.095
Courts	26%	0%	11%	.082
Lawyers	5%	0%	5%	—
Finances (r_α = .280)	0.5* (0.7)	0.1 (0.4)	0.1* (0.1)	**.025**
Collection Agency	37%	14%	11%	—
Storekeepers	11%	0%	0%	—
Social welfare workers	5%	0%	0%	—
Workplace (r_α = .489)	0.4 (0.7)	0.0 (0.0)	0.4 (0.6)	.082
Work supervisor	21%	0%	32%	.073
Co-workers	16%	0%	11%	
Family and friends (r_α = .286)	0.5 (0.8)	0.1 (0.4)	0.4 (0.7)	—
Spouse	5%	7%	11%	—
Family members	21%	0%	16%	—
Friends	11%	7%	16%	—
Roommates or neighbors	10%	0%	0%	—

Note. n = 52 unless otherwise indicated. The chi-square statistic tests differences in percentages; the analysis of variance tests differences in means (followed by standard deviations in parentheses). The associated p-value is reported if less than .100. One group value in a row is starred if different from the other two at $p < .05$; two group values in a row are starred if different from each other at $p < .05$.

[a]Reported membership in any of the following: church group, sports team/club, professional association, special interest group, music/band/choir, or community social group.

[b]Items were these: learn new skills, do well in educational activities, try out new experiences, do well at a school or work task, keep a job or stay in school, get along with people at work or school, work or study hard all day, follow through on plans, keep trying to work on a problem, do what you know is right, feel close to family and friends, and help other people. The items were scored 1 = not easy, 2 = sort of easy, 3 = easy, 4 = very easy.

Figure 2

IRRITATION SOURCES BY CURRICULUM GROUP

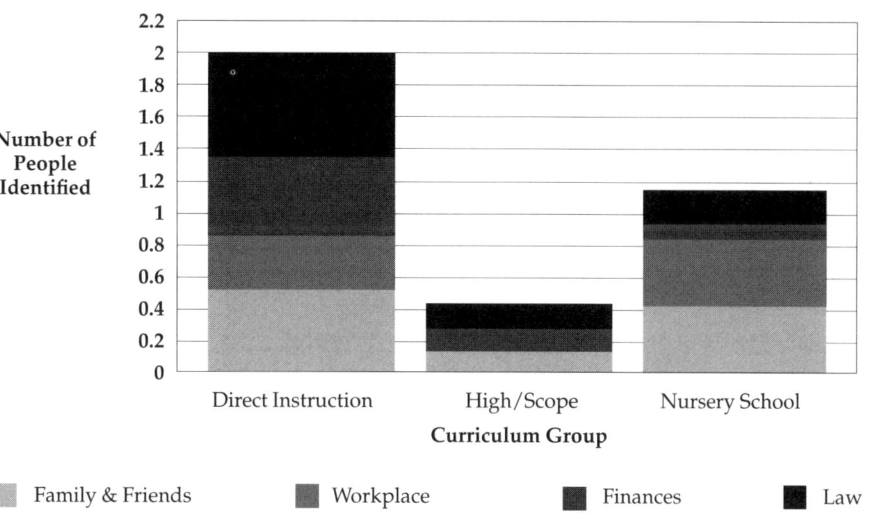

giving you a hard time lately"). On a 12-item scale identifying various categories of people, members of the Direct Instruction group identified an average of 2.0 persons, while members of the High/Scope group identified an average of 0.4 persons. Table 10 indicates the various categories into which the sources of irritation fell. The Direct Instruction group identified significantly more sources of irritation in *finances* than the Nursery School group did, and the curriculum groups differed nearly significantly in their number of sources of irritation in *law* and in the *workplace*. Within these broad categories, the most frequently named individual sources of irritation were collection agencies, work supervisors, police, courts, and family members, in that order. The prominence of police and courts, particularly for the Direct Instruction group members, corroborates the findings about that group's felony arrests, as reported on pp. 50–58. At age 15, the curriculum groups did not differ significantly from one another in their answers to a similar 11-item sources-of-irritation question; the correlation between the age-15 ratings and the age-23 ratings was only .111 (n = 42), suggesting that the sources of irritation that people identify vary according to their age and life situation.

Five-Year Plans

As an answer to the question "Where do you expect your income to come from 5 years from now?", 94% of the sample (n = 52) identified their own job; curriculum groups did not differ significantly on this item. Other 5-year life goals identified by at least 10% of the sample (n = 52) included owning a home (42%); achieving more schooling (31%); owning a car or other possessions (21%); getting married (21%); achieving work success (17%); being a good parent (14%); travel, moving, or adventure (14%); and having children

(12%). The curriculum groups did not differ significantly on any of these variables.

Positives and Negatives of Life

At least 10% of the respondents identified the following positive aspects of their lives: job/career (29%), own children/new family (25%), marriage/spouse (12%), car (10%), and independence (10%); 33% added that they were satisfied with themselves. At least 10% of the respondents identified the following difficulties and frustrations in their lives: financial problems (17%), work-related problems (12%), unemployment/no steady job (10%), drug use/personal or community problems (10%), no difficulties (10%). Curriculum groups did not differ significantly on any of these variables.

Misconduct and Crime

Misconduct

As previously reported (Schweinhart et al., 1986b) and as shown in Table 11, the High/Scope group at age 15 reported significantly fewer acts of misconduct than did the Direct Instruction group. The High/Scope group reported an average of only 5.9 acts of misconduct (the average sum of scores on 18 items) as compared with the 14.9 acts of misconduct reported by the Direct Instruction group.[8] When age-15 respondents scored the same 18 items of misconduct in the High/Scope Perry Preschool Project, the program group reported an average of 5.2 acts of misconduct, and the no-program group reported an average of 7.1 acts of misconduct. Because sample members in the High/Scope Perry Project had background characteristics similar to those of the sample members in the Curriculum Comparison Study, the age-15 misconduct data from the two studies suggests that the Direct Instruction group in the Preschool Curriculum Comparison Study committed twice as many acts of misconduct as they would have, had they attended no preschool program at all.

At age 23, in an analysis of variance, the curriculum groups did not differ significantly in how they scored on a 14-item list of misconduct that was quite similar to the age-15 list. However, curriculum groups had significantly unequal variances as tested by the Levene test, which means that rather than analysis of variance, the Kruskal-Wallis chi-square analysis of groups' mean ranks is the appropriate analysis to employ.[9] By this test, on

[8]These numbers differ from those reported by Schweinhart et al. (1986b), because the scale was recalibrated to obtain the scores in Table 11; "3 or 4 times" was scored as 3.5 instead of as 3, and "5 or more times" was scored as 5 instead of 4.

[9]For most variables, however, the analysis of variance yielded the same results as the Kruskal-Wallis statistic despite unequal group variances.

Table 11

GROUP COMPARISONS OF SELF-REPORTED MISCONDUCT

Variable	Direct Instruction	High/ Scope	Nursery School	p
Misconduct at age 15 (mean sum of scores on 18 items[a]; $r_\alpha = .788$)	14.9* (14.7)	5.9* (6.1)	8.0 (9.1)	**.036**
Mean rank	*32.8*	*24.1*	*25.6*	—
Misconduct at age 23 (mean sum of scores on 14 items[b]; $r_\alpha = .748$)	8.7 (9.0)	5.3 (7.4)	9.9 (6.6)	—
Mean rank	*27.0*	*18.7**	*31.8**	**.049**
Times suspended from high school	1.6 (1.5)	1.3 (1.3)	0.8 (1.0)	—
% suspended 0 times	37%	29%	48%	
% suspended 1–2 times	32%	50%	42%	
% suspended 3 or more times	32%	21%	11%	
Ever expelled from high school	16%	7%	5%	—
Times suspended from work (n = 51)	0.6 (1.1)	0.1 (0.3)	0.0 0.0	**.053**
Mean rank	*30.4**	*25.3*	*23.5**	**.033**
Suspended from work				
% suspended 1 time	16%	7%	0%	
% suspended 3 or more times	11%	0%	0%	
Times picked up or arrested[c]	1.0 (1.2)	0.4 (0.9)	0.8 (1.5)	—

Note. $n = 52$ unless otherwise indicated. The chi-square statistic tests differences in percentages; the analysis of variance tests differences in means (followed by standard deviations in parentheses); the Kruskal-Wallis H statistic tests differences in mean ranks (in italics). The associated p-value is reported if less than .100. One group value in a row is starred if different from the other two at $p < .05$; two group values in a row are starred if different from each other at $p < .05$.

[a]The 18 items were: hit an instructor/supervisor, had a serious fight in school or at work, been in a group fight, seriously injured someone, used a weapon to get something, committed arson, purposely damaged school property, purposely damaged work property, stole something worth under $50, stole something worth over $50, stole something from a store, stole a car, stole part of a car, smoked marijuana, used other illegal drugs, argued or fought with parents, ran away from home, and trespassed. The items were scored 0 (for never), 1 (for once), 2 (for twice), 3.5 (for 3 to 4 times), and 5 (for 5 or more times).

[b]The 14 items were: gotten into a serious fight at work or at school, involved in a family fight, in fight with a group of friends against another group, injured someone so they needed medical care, used a weapon to get something from a person, took something worth less than $50, took something worth more than $50, took car from someone outside your family, broke into a house or building, set fire to property, damaged property, smoked marijuana, and used other drugs. Items were scored as explained in footnote *a*. The Pearson correlation coefficient between self-reported misconduct at age 15 and self-reported misconduct at age 23 was .531 ($n = 42$, $p < .001$).

[c]Respondents reported being picked up or arrested 0.8 times on average, only 40% of the average of 2.0 actual arrests listed in juvenile and adult arrest records; the Pearson correlation coefficient between the two variables was .358 ($n = 52$, $p = .009$)

the same 14-item list of misconduct, the mean rank of the High/Scope group was significantly lower than the mean rank of the Nursery School group.

Other Types of Misconduct

Regarding suspensions from work, the Direct Instruction group had a significantly higher mean rank than did the Nursery School group, reflecting the fact that 27% of Direct Instruction group members versus none of Nursery School group members had ever been suspended from work. Curriculum groups did not differ significantly in the number of times they reported being suspended from high school, being expelled from high school, or being picked up or arrested. While curriculum group differences in self-reported misconduct are corroborated by similar differences in felony arrests, respondents underreported the numbers of their arrests: They reported an average of only 0.8 arrests, whereas a search of juvenile and adult arrest records revealed an average of 2.0 actual arrests.

Lifetime Arrests

As shown in Figure 3 and Table 12, the Direct Instruction group experienced over twice as many *lifetime arrests,* including over twice as many *adult arrests,* as either of the other two curriculum groups — a nearly significant difference for both variables. The Direct Instruction group averaged 3.2 lifetime arrests, as compared with 1.5 for the High/Scope group and 1.3 for the Nursery School group. In the High/Scope Perry Preschool Project, the estimated average lifetime arrests by age 23 were 1.8 for the program

Figure 3

MEAN ARRESTS THROUGH AGE 23 BY CURRICULUM GROUP

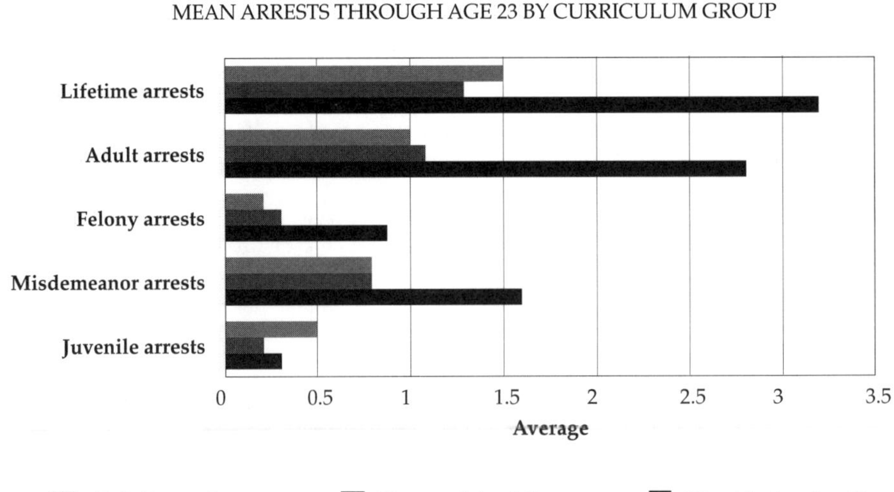

Table 12

GROUP COMPARISONS OF ARREST RECORDS

Variable	Direct Instruction	High/ Scope	Nursery School	*p*
Lifetime arrests (juvenile and adult))	3.2 (4.0)	1.5 (2.6)	1.3 (2.5)	.083
% having 1–4	39%	32%	30%	
% having 5–14	26%	14%	9%	
Adult arrests (felonies and misdemeanors)	2.8 (3.9)	1.0 (2.1)	1.1 (2.0)	.053
% having 1–4	35%	32%	30%	
% having 5–12	22%	5%	9%	
Total felony arrests	0.9 (1.3)	0.2 (0.7)	0.3 (0.8)	**.040**
% having 1–2	22%	5%	13%	
% having 3–4	17%	5%	4%	
Felony arrests at ages 17–21	0.3 (0.5)	0.1 (0.2)	0.3 (0.9)	—
Felony arrests at age 22 and over	0.6* (0.9)	0.1 (0.6)	0.1 (0.3)	**.039**
Misdemeanors	2.0 (2.9)	0.8 (1.6)	0.8 (1.4)	—
% having 1–4	26%	27%	30%	
% having 5–9	13%	5%	4%	
Juvenile arrests	0.3 (0.7)	0.5 (1.7)	0.2 (0.7)	—
% having 1–3	22%	9%	4%	
% having 8	0%	5%	0%	
Ever convicted of felony & sentenced to prison	13%	5%	9%	—
Average minimum months of felony prison sentences (n = 68)	4.2 (9.6)	0.8 (3.8)	5.0 (16.7)	—
Average maximum months of felony prison sentences (n = 68)	31.3 (78.6)	8.2 (38.4)	15.1 (53.9)	—
Months of probation for misdemeanors	0.3	0.8	0.3	—
Juvenile offense adjudications	0.1 (0.3)	0.3 (1.3)	0.1 (0.5)	—

Note. $n = 68$ unless otherwise indicated. The chi-square statistic tests differences in percentages; the analysis of variance tests differences in means (followed by standard deviations in parentheses). The associated p-value is reported if less than .100. One group value in a row is starred if different from the other two at $p < .05$; two group values in a row are starred if different from each other at $p < .05$.

group and 3.5 for the no-program group.[10] This comparison suggests that the Direct Instruction program did not lead to *more* arrests than would have occurred without the program, but neither did it lead to *fewer* arrests, as did the other preschool programs.

Felony Arrests

Most important, compared with each of the other two curriculum groups, the Direct Instruction group experienced significantly more *felony arrests.* They averaged three times as many total felony arrests as either of the other two groups, and significant differences also appeared in *felony arrests at age 22 and over,* when the numbers of such arrests became more substantial; the average for these years was four times as many. As Figure 4 and Table 12 show, 39% of the Direct Instruction group members had felony arrest records, as compared with only 10% of the High/Scope group and 17% of the Nursery School group. This finding represents a much more important corroboration of the finding on age-15 self-reported misconduct than the similar finding on age-23 self-reported misconduct provides, simply because arrests are the official recognition of crime, the indication that the justice system has actually had to deal with the problem. This entire pattern has a precedent in the High/Scope Perry Preschool Project. In that study, a significant median difference between the program group and the no-program group in age-15 *self-reported misconduct* (Schweinhart & Weikart, 1980) preceded large and significant group differences in *arrest rates* at these later ages.

Felony Arrests and Geographic Stability

In Table 12, the stated differences between curriculum groups in felony arrests are based on the complete original sample of 68 persons. This is because the lack of an arrest record for a study participant is not considered to be missing data (as the absence of a school record would be); rather it is an indication that the study participant experienced no arrests. It may be argued, however, that a finding of *no arrest* in a particular jurisdiction is only meaningful for persons who reside in that jurisdiction, specifically, for persons who had the opportunity to commit a crime and be arrested in that jurisdiction. We do not have precise data on when sample members lived in Washtenaw County, but we do know that all of them lived there as children. We also know that according to the current-residence question on the age-23 interview, 43 still lived in Michigan, while 6 lived elsewhere, and 19 were not found. To decide whether the curriculum group differences in felony arrests were due to differential geographic stability, we examined the variable for the three curriculum subgroups known to be still living in Michigan

[10]Because age 23 is halfway between ages 19 and 27, these numbers average the arrests at age 19 and at age 27. The estimate assumes that arrests take place at the same annual frequency from ages 19 to 27.

Figure 4

FELONY ARRESTS BY CURRICULUM GROUP

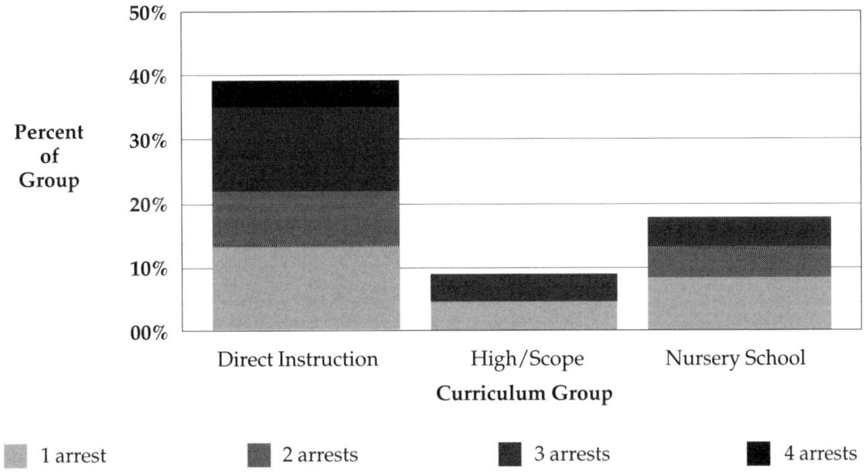

Percent of Group

50%
40%
30%
20%
10%
00%

Direct Instruction
High/Scope
Nursery School

Curriculum Group

1 arrest
2 arrests
3 arrests
4 arrests

at age 23. The group means for the Michigan subgroups were nearly identical to those of the complete groups:

- For the Direct Instruction group, 1.0 in the Michigan subgroup versus 0.9 in the complete group
- For the High/Scope group, 0.3 versus 0.2
- For the Nursery School group, 0.5 versus 0.3

These subgroup findings suggest that differential geographic stability does not account for the substantial felony arrest differences between the Direct Instruction group and the High/Scope group.

Felony Arrests and Gender

The group differences in felony arrests were also not attributable to gender. A two-way analysis of variance found statistically significant effects for curriculum group ($p = .032$) and gender ($p = .016$) but not for the interaction of group and gender. Overall and in each curriculum group, males had more felony arrests than females.

Felony Arrests and Preschool Program Duration

In his critique of this study's findings through age 15, Bereiter (1986) suggested that the curriculum group difference in misconduct might be due to the fact that the first cohort of 8 members of the Direct Instruction group (and 8 members of the Nursery School group) attended only 1 year of the preschool program, whereas all of the High/Scope group attended for 2 years. To see if the shorter preschool programs influenced the curriculum group difference in felony arrests, we conducted the analysis with the subsample who attended their preschool programs for 2 years. As with the geographical stability analysis, the pattern remained the same.

- For the Direct Instruction group, 0.9 in the 2-year subgroup versus 0.9 in the original group
- For the High/Scope group, 0.2 versus 0.2
- For the Nursery School group, 0.4 versus 0.3

We can conclude from this analysis of subgroups that differential preschool program duration does not account for the substantial group differences in felony arrests.

Other Arrests and Adjudications

While curriculum groups did not differ significantly in either adult misdemeanors or juvenile arrests, the Direct Instruction group members were arrested for misdemeanors twice as often as members of either of the other curriculum groups. The curriculum groups did not differ significantly in the low-incidence events of felony convictions, prison sentences, months of probation, days in jail, fines for misdemeanors, or adjudications for juvenile offenses. The minimum and maximum felony sentences for the Direct Instruction group were, however, considerably longer than those for the High/Scope group. Again, as with the High/Scope Perry Preschool Project, the significant group differences were found in arrest rates, not in any judicial processing following the arrests. Larger samples (or tighter distributions) are necessary to find significant differences in these criminal justice actions, which are experienced only rarely by people in the general population.

Types of Crimes

As Figure 5 and Table 13 (on p. 58) show, the Direct Instruction group was arrested for significantly more *property felonies* than the other two curriculum groups and for significantly more *property misdemeanors* than the High/Scope group. (In Figure 5, "crimes" include felonies and misdemeanors.) Property felonies are breaking and entering, arson, larceny over $100, receiving or concealing stolen property over $100, fraudulent activities, larceny from a person, and vehicle theft. Property misdemeanors are larceny under $100 (including larceny from a building and shoplifting), malicious destruction of property under $100, receiving or concealing stolen property, and fraud. The High/Scope Perry Preschool Project found a similar,

Figure 5

MEAN ARRESTS FOR SPECIFIC TYPES OF FELONIES/MISDEMEANORS THROUGH AGE 23 BY CURRICULUM GROUP

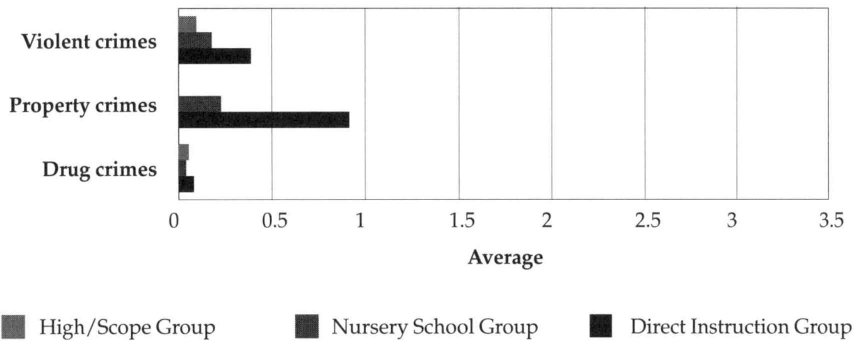

nearly significant difference between the program group and the no-program group, at age 27, in property crimes (means of 0.6 vs. 1.3, $p = .073$).

Curriculum groups did not differ significantly in felonies or misdemeanors involving violence against persons or in drug-related felonies. Following the pattern of the group differences in general types of felony arrests, the Direct Instruction group had a significantly higher mean rank on the number of specific types of felonies cited at arrest than the High/Scope group did; the Direct Instruction group also had a nearly significantly higher mean rank on this variable. In particular, Direction Instruction group members were cited significantly more often than the High/Scope and Nursery School curriculum groups for *assault with a dangerous weapon;* indeed, 17% of the Direct Instruction group members were cited for assault with a dangerous weapon, whereas no one in the High/Scope group or Nursery School group was cited for this crime.

Interviewer Ratings of Respondents

After the age-23 interview, the interviewer rated each respondent from 1 to 7 on each of 13 items, with 7 being the high end of the scale; the 13 items were these: cooperative, sociable, involved, talkative, attentive, active, relaxed, quick to respond, keeps trying, self-confident, open, truthful, and warm. The alpha coefficient for the ratings was .848. The mean score for the full sample was 6.4 ($SD = 0.7$, $n = 52$); the mean scores of the three curriculum groups did not differ significantly from one another. Neither did they differ significantly in their mean scores on an additional item — "truthfulness of misconduct responses." On this item, the full sample's mean score was 1.2 ($SD = 0.5$, $n = 52$), with 1 = completely honest, 2 = honest after encouragement from interviewer, 3 = may be exaggerated or otherwise distorted, 4 = likely to be false. The absence of significant differences across curriculum groups constitutes evidence not only that the groups appeared to be honest but also that the interviewer was not biased by chance for or against any curriculum group.

Table 13

GROUP COMPARISONS OF TYPES OF CRIMES FROM ARREST RECORDS

Variable	Direct Instruction	High/ Scope	Nursery School	p
General types of felonies				
Property	0.52* (0.90)	0.00 (0.00)	0.09 (0.42)	**.007**
Personal violence	0.09 (0.42)	0.05 (0.21)	0.04 (0.21)	—
Drug-related	0.09 (0.29)	0.05 (0.21)	0.04 (0.21)	—
Specific types of felonies (mean count on 18 items; r_α = .806)	1.0 (1.5)	0.2 (0.7)	0.5 (1.2)	.066
Mean rank	*40.4**	*29.9**	*33.0*	**.043**
Assault with a dangerous weapon	17%*	0%	0%	**.016**
Dangerous drugs	9%	5%	4%	—
Aggravated assault and/or battery	9%	0%	4%	—
Breaking and entering	4%	5%	4%	—
Armed robbery	4%	5%	4%	—
Arson	9%	0%	0%	—
Carry a concealed weapon	9%	0%	0%	—
Larceny over $100	4%	0%	4%	—
Receiving/concealing stolen property over $100	0%	5%	4%	—
Assault intending great bodily harm	0%	0%	4%	—
Escape	4%	0%	0%	—
Firearm misdemeanor in a felony arrest	4%	0%	0%	—
Fraudulent activities	4%	0%	0%	—
Larceny from a person	4%	0%	0%	—
Motor theft misdemeanor in a felony arrest	4%	0%	0%	—
Murder	4%	0%	0%	—
Vehicle theft	0%	0%	4%	—
General types of misdemeanors				
Property	0.39* (0.84)	0.00* (0.00)	0.13 (0.34)	**.046**
Personal violence	0.30 (0.88)	0.05 (0.21)	0.13 (0.34)	—

Note. n = 68 unless otherwise indicated. The chi-square statistic tests differences in percentages; the analysis of variance tests differences in means (followed by standard deviations in parentheses); the Kruskal-Wallis H statistic tests differences in mean ranks (in italics). The associated p-value is reported if less than .100. One group value in a row is starred if different from the other two at $p < .05$; two group values in a row are starred if different from each other at $p < .05$.

Summary of Findings at Age 23

Table 14 (on p. 60) presents all of the statistically significant ($p < .05$) differences between curriculum groups on variables studied at age 23. Because the groups were significantly different on only a few variables through age 10 and at age 15, it is striking that at age 23, they were significantly different on 20 variables. We do not interpret these new findings as delayed effects but rather as the expression of enduring tendencies that were present but not measured (perhaps could not have been measured) at an earlier age.

In summarizing the findings of this study, it is useful to consider the 12 possible ways in which three curriculum groups can have statistically significant differences on a variable. First, any one of the three groups can have a significant advantage over one or both of the other two groups (9 possible situations). Second, any two of the groups can have a significant advantage over the remaining group (3 possible situations).[11]

One general empirical finding of this study eliminated 5 of these possible situations: **There is no variable on which the Direct Instruction group had a statistically significant advantage over either or both of the other curriculum groups.** The 20 variables on which curriculum groups differed significantly at age 23 present 6 of the 7 remaining possible advantageous situations.[12]

On 17 of the 20 variables in Table 14, the High/Scope or the Nursery School group or both had a statistically significant advantage over the Direct Instruction group. The High/Scope and Nursery School groups both had the following significant advantages over the Direct Instruction group, three of which involve felonies:

- Fewer felony arrests at age 22 and over
- Fewer property-type felonies
- Fewer assaults with a dangerous weapon
- Fewer years of special education for emotional impairment or disturbance
- More participation in volunteer work
- More ownership of recent-model cars

The High/Scope group had the following significant advantages over the Direct Instruction group:

- Lower total number of felony arrests

---

[11]The Bonferroni post-hoc analysis used in this study permits the anomalous situation in which, despite an overall significant difference across the groups, no specific group has a significant advantage over any other group. In this situation, we make the logical assumption that the two extreme groups are significantly different from each other.

[12]There were no instances of the situation in which the Nursery School group had a significant advantage over both the Direct Instruction group and the High/Scope group.

Table 14

SUMMARY OF STATISTICALLY SIGNIFICANT ($p < .05$) AGE-23 FINDINGS

Variable	*n*	Direct Instruction	High/ Scope	Nursery School
Felony arrests at age 22 and over	68	0.6*	0.1	0.1
Property-type felonies	68	0.5*	0.0	0.1
Assault with a dangerous weapon	68	17%*	0%	0%
Years of special education for emotional impairment or disturbance	46	1.1*	0.1	0.1
Ever done volunteer work	52	11%*	43%	44%
Recent (vs. older) car	28	8%*	57%	78%
Total felony arrests	68	0.9	0.2	0.3
***Mean rank* on "specific types of felonies"**	68	*40.4**	*29.9**	*33.0*
Property-type misdemeanors	68	0.4*	0.0*	0.1
Sources of irritation	52	2.0*	0.4*	1.2
Highest year of schooling planned	44	14.1*	16.3*	15.1
Spouse living in respondent's household	49	0%*	31%*	18%
Checking account	50	11%*	46%*	17%
***Mean rank* on "times suspended from work"**	52	*30.4**	*25.3*	*23.5**
Location of current home	49			
Ypsilanti		84%*	64%	44%*
Rest of Washtenaw County		5%	0%	25%
Rest of Michigan		0%	14%	25%
Rest of U.S.		11%	21%	6%
Voted in last presidential election	52	21%	62%*	22%
Times dropped out and returned to school	46	0.00	0.14	0.00
***Mean rank* on "misconduct at 23"**	52	*27.0*	*18.7**	*31.8**
Years of compensatory education	46	0.3	0.6*	0.0*
Past year's earnings of respondent	45	$5,769	$3,738*	$8,881*

Note. The chi-square statistic tests differences in percentages; the analysis of variance tests differences in means (standard deviations appear in the source tables); the Kruskal-Wallis *H* statistic tests differences in mean ranks (in italics). One group value in a row is starred if different from the other two at $p < .05$; two group values in a row are starred if different from each other at $p < .05$.

- Lower mean rank on specific types of felonies
- Fewer property-type misdemeanors
- Fewer people in the community seen as sources of irritation
- Higher level of schooling planned
- More married, living with their spouses
- More with checking accounts

The Nursery School group had the following significant advantages over the Direct Instruction group:

- Lower mean rank on suspensions from work
- Greater geographic mobility

The High/Scope group had the following significant advantages over the Direct Instruction group and the Nursery School group:

- More voting in the last presidential election
- More returning to high school after dropping out

On three of the remaining variables, either the High/Scope group had a significant advantage over the Nursery School group, or vice versa. In addition to the two advantageous differences just mentioned, the High/Scope group had one other significant advantage over the Nursery School group:

- Lower mean rank on acts of misconduct reported at age 23

The Nursery School group had two significant advantages over the High/Scope group:

- Fewer years of compensatory education
- Higher average annual earnings at age 23

From the perspective of the sheer number of statistically significant findings, **the strongest conclusion from this study is that the Nursery School group and especially the High/Scope group had significant advantages over the Direct Instruction group at age 23.** Although some of the significant findings involve areas of advantage that overlap (e.g., fewer felony arrests and fewer felony arrests at age 22 and over), we can cite 17 findings that fully support this conclusion. In contrast, only 2 findings support the conclusion that the Nursery School group had significant advantages over the High/Scope group, while 3 findings support the opposite conclusion.

IV Implications of the Study Findings

The High/Scope study of the effects of three different preschool curriculum models was initiated in the late 1960s, after the first 5 years of data from the High/Scope Perry Preschool Project had indicated that high-quality early childhood education could have a positive effect on children's development. This encouraging finding opened the question of curriculum model effectiveness. Which method should be used when implementing early education programs to achieve the best results? Did one theoretical approach have an advantage over another, either in the short term or in the long term? Perhaps different approaches contributed to different areas of children's development or to different skills. With these questions in mind, we decided to study the effects of curriculum models representing three of the basic approaches shown in Figure 1 on page 25.

Educational writings at that time, especially Maya Pines's widely circulated article on Direct Instruction (Pines, 1967), led us to choose the Direct Instruction model to represent the "teacher-initiates/child-responds" category. The obvious choice to represent the "teacher-responds/child-initiates" category was the traditional Nursery School approach, which was at that time the most widely used approach to educating young children. To complete the study, we selected the High/Scope Curriculum to represent the "teacher-initiates/child-initiates" category. Not only was this a curriculum model that had been successfully implemented in the High/Scope Perry Preschool Project, but it was also a model that a growing number of sites around the country were interested in using. For three reasons, the Montessori model was not included in the study: The cost of materials establishing a Montessori program was high, availability of Montessori-trained staff who were state-certified teachers was limited, and Montessori's blend of child-centeredness and prescribed use of didactic materials made it a mix of two of the four major theoretical approaches.

For the study to achieve its goals, each model's implementation had to adhere to the highest standards of model quality. The process of setting up the High/Scope class was straightforward, because staff with the necessary skills were readily available. The traditional Nursery School class was easily staffed as well — with two teachers who had experience teaching nursery school and also a master's degree in early childhood education. The Direct Instruction class was the most difficult to establish. To prepare to implement the class, teaching staff visited Direct Instruction's demonstration program at its home site at the University of Illinois and participated in training conducted in Ypsilanti by their consultants. Once the three programs were established, outside observers verified the quality of the programs and their adherence to their respective curriculum models. The random assignment of children to curriculum groups gave the study strong internal validity, which served as a rationale for the follow-ups at ages 15 and 23. Over three fourths of the original study participants were found and interviewed at each follow-up.

Based on the initial findings of this study, Weikart et al. (1978) reached the following conclusions:

> Of the three major preschool models compared in [this] Project, all were effective and none was more so than another. . . .
>
> The fact that any well delivered curriculum will lead to improved performance on measures of aptitude and achievement in school does not

> imply, however, that these curricula will lead to other identical ends. When it comes to the question of how best to develop the more global competencies and aptitudes that characterize a productive and rewarding adult life, we confront once again the problem of determining which pedagogical practices are most likely to contribute to these ends. (p. 136)

These statements held out the possibility of long-term differences in curriculum effects even in the absence of identified short-term differences. That possibility has now been realized.

The interpretation of the findings and implications of this study revolve around two comparisons — first, Direct Instruction versus the other two curriculum models; and second, the High/Scope model versus the Nursery School model.

Direct Instruction's Failure to Prevent Crime

The pattern of results for study participants at age 15, and now at age 23, clearly identifies major long-term consequences of using Direct Instruction in preschool programs. Compared with the High/Scope and Nursery School groups, *the Direct Instruction group had no significant advantages and various significant disadvantages — most striking was the finding that the Direct Instruction group had three times as many felony arrests, and especially more arrests for property felonies.* There were additional signs that, compared with the other two curriculum groups, the Direct Instruction group had more difficulty fitting into the community: They had greater need for special education for emotional impairment and participated less in volunteer work. Compared with the High/Scope group, the Direct Instruction group perceived five times as many people in the community as sources of irritation and had less ambitious educational plans; fewer (in fact none) of the Direct Instruction group members were living with their spouses (or married). The Nursery School group had fewer work suspensions and greater geographic mobility than the Direct Instruction group, and compared with the Direct Instruction group's on-time high school graduation rate of only 47%, the Nursery School group had a 72% on-time-graduation rate. This graduation rate difference was not a significant one, but the pattern was almost exactly the same as that found in the Illinois study (Karnes et al., 1983), which is the only other study that has examined whether different preschool curriculum models have varying effects on high school graduation.

It is extremely unlikely that this pattern of life-adjustment difficulties is accidental. Although the sample size in this study was small, it was large enough that these group differences achieved statistical significance. The point of testing for statistical significance is to guard against attributing meaning to accidental findings. On the other hand, 1 out of 20 findings could be significant with a probability of .05 on the basis of chance alone. Several of the curriculum group significant differences — in numbers of recent-model car owners and numbers having checking accounts, for example — may be spurious in this way, because they appear to form no logical pattern (although perhaps the causal paths leading to such differences are simply difficult to understand). But the basic finding that the Direct Instruction group is more often arrested for felonies than the other curriculum groups is logically consistent with several other findings, including self-reported misconduct at age 15 and misconduct and arrest data at age 23. The felony arrest finding also stands up to methodological challenges, such as the contention that it is due to the curriculum groups' differential geographic stability (see the discussion of this point on p. 54). Furthermore, felony arrests are real-world data, representing not merely a single psychological score that might be swayed by a bad assessment-session, but rather the collective, independent judgments of many law enforcement officials over years of time.

A Closer Look at Instructional Practices That Prevent Crime

What could explain this pattern of crime and misconduct findings? Having decision-making power and control of one's environment in early childhood (which was the experience of children in the High/Scope and Nursery School programs but not of those in the Direct Instruction program) appears to have led to a capability for more-disciplined behavior in adulthood. A closer look at the differences between the three curriculums (introduced on p. 25) may shed some light on this conclusion.

Direct Instruction is rooted in learning theory and behavior modification, which derive their educational objectives from the analysis of the subject matter to be learned. Teachers precisely adhere to manuals; they transmit knowledge to children and expect them to follow directions without question. The children use workbooks that precisely specify the exercises necessary to achieve the learning objectives. In contrast, the High/Scope and Nursery School models are rooted in child development theory and the traditions of early childhood education, which derive their educational objectives from the observation and analysis of children's development. Teachers construct settings in which children design and carry out their own learning activities.

In the study, systematic observation of the three classrooms confirmed these differences: Direct Instruction children spent 72% of their time involved in *teacher-defined activities,* while High/Scope children spent 48% of their time and Nursery School children spent 56% of their time in this way (Weikart et al., 1978). Direct Instruction children spent only 2% of their time participating in *child-defined activities, fantasy, and role-play,* whereas High/Scope children spent 27% of their time and Nursery School children spent 21% of their time in these ways.

Unlike their High/Scope and Nursery School counterparts, who learned that adults and peers provide support and encouragement, the Direct Instruction children learned that they had little control over their lives. As adults, they engaged in more property crimes, showing a lack of respect for the property of others, and they identified more kinds of people in the community who "gave them a hard time." Direct Instruction during their early childhood years did nothing to dispel the lesson that many children living in poverty learn — that they are not in charge of their lives, others are. They failed to learn vital social and decision-making skills (which are developed by programs emphasizing child-initiated learning activities) — skills that would permit them to assume responsibility for their lives as they moved from the dependence of childhood to the independence of adolescence and adulthood. Once given a chance to decide and control, they had a stronger tendency to strike out at those in their way and to see others as obstacles. All they had to show for a year or two of intense drill and practice in early childhood was an ephemeral advantage in intellectual performance at the end of the preschool program. They had none of the lasting benefits associated with high-quality preschool programs.

In light of the benefits that children might obtain from being enrolled in early childhood programs emphasizing child initiative, the increase in felony arrests might well be considered a harmful effect of providing a Direct Instruction program for young children living in poverty. This study does not show that Direct Instruction *increased* felonies. Indeed, comparison with the High/Scope Perry Preschool Project findings (where sample members had similar background characteristics) suggests that the Direct Instruction group members were arrested for about as many felonies as they would have been if the group had not attended a preschool program. This curriculum comparison study does, however, offer evidence that Direct Instruction *does not prevent* felony arrests as well as High/Scope or Nursery School education.

A logical problem with this finding would seem to be this: How can a person's sense of control, or self-determination, be so readily altered in early childhood and yet be impervious to later environmental influences? The explanation may be that early childhood is a sensitive period in children's development. Bereiter (1986) argued that any feelings children had about lacking control of their lives could not possibly persist in the face of improved intellectual performance and school achievement — an argument that loses much of its force in light of the finding that Direct Instruction's intellectual improvements have proved ephemeral in this and other studies. But on this point the research diverges, with Direct Instruction researchers finding that Direct Instruction programs lead to lasting academic improvements, while independent researchers find that the Direct Instruction program's effects on intellectual performance and school achievement fade away.

Implications for Teacher-Directed Instructional Practices

It is hard to say how much research of the sort presented here is needed to answer the question of which preschool curriculum has the most-lasting benefits. For scientific purposes, educational research questions are never fully answered. Studies proceed not by confirming hypotheses, but by ruling out alternate hypotheses — and even these decisions are reached with statistical probability rather than absolute certainty. For practical purposes, however, educators must at some point act on the weight of the evidence that existing studies provide. Although the High/Scope Preschool Curriculum Comparison Study — with its random assignment to curriculum groups and satisfactory sample retention after 20 years — is very valuable, such studies are rare because they are extremely difficult to conduct. Because this study is carefully done and has lasted two decades, and because no other study like it is under way, practitioners should pay attention to its findings. If they are not guided by the evidence of studies such as this one, they may be guided by no scientific evidence at all.

This study — primarily through its examination of arrest records — shows that compared with preschool curriculum models that emphasize child initiative, Direct Instruction fails to have beneficial effects on the long-term social development of participants. These findings are so far uncorroborated, since neither the Louisville study, the Illinois study, nor any other long-term preschool curriculum comparison study has examined arrest records. Nevertheless, our arrest findings do provide a fair test of the question. Thus, preschool teachers who use Direct Instruction with young children living in poverty are pursuing a risky path in ignoring the very important role that a high-quality preschool curriculum can play in children's social development. On a recent mail-in survey of NAEYC members reported by Epstein, Schweinhart, and McAdoo (1996), 13% of respondents said they used Direct Instruction in their classrooms. Because the National Association for the Education of Young Children has clearly opposed the use of such programs, this percentage may underestimate the prevalence of Direct Instruction in the nation's preschool classrooms, which include many preschool teachers not belonging to NAEYC.

Several possible generalizations of this study's finding about social development deserve serious consideration. For example, should the findings be generalized to other forms of teacher-directed instruction, including those used with young children who have disabilities and those used in early elementary education?

First, it seems reasonable to assume that the negative social findings associated with Direct Instruction in this study are more extreme than any related findings that might be associated with ordinary teacher-directed instruction. Like all teacher-directed instruction, Direct Instruction places the teacher in control of learning activities in the classroom, but Direct Instruction is more intense and tightly scripted. For this reason, we believe that Direct Instruction techniques should be used sparingly if at all with children who have disabilities; while such techniques may lead to success on short-term objectives, they do not help children to develop a sense of control of their lives — something that is especially important for children with disabilities.

Second, it seems reasonable to assume that as young children first experience preschool or kindergarten, they are more sensitive to the social effects of instructional methods than they will be when they are older. Because they are just learning the way the world outside their family works, a particular instructional practice may leave a stronger impression on them than it leaves on older children. Thus, this study calls for taking a second look at the effects of ordinary teacher-directed instruction in preschool and early elementary classes.

The finding of a relationship between preschool program experience and felony arrests two decades later presents a strong argument that instructional methods can convey powerful lifetime lessons to young, impressionable students. Given our grave national concern about crime and our near-despair about how to prevent it, it would be a wise precaution for school districts concerned about students' progress and program effects to examine students' misconduct and criminal arrests just as closely as they now examine their achievement test scores. School programs may be one of society's best hopes for preventing and reducing crime by counteracting rather than reenforcing young people's sense of inefficacy and despair.

Curriculum Models and Program Quality

What can be said about the differences between the High/Scope group and the Nursery School group? Compared with the High/Scope group, the Nursery School group started with significantly more-educated mothers (a selection bias that could to some extent account for later apparent program effects). After the preschool program, the Nursery School group spent fewer years in compensatory education and had higher average annual earnings at age 23 than the High/Scope group. On the other hand, compared with the Nursery School group, the High/Scope group had a lower mean rank on acts of misconduct at age 23 and more members voting in the last presidential election. The lack of a clear-cut pattern of advantage for one or the other curriculum group suggests that both programs had the ingredients essential to children's long-term success — support for children's initiative, choice, and independent decision-making.

This study implies that a teacher's choice of a specific curriculum model is the key to providing a high-quality preschool program that produces lasting benefits. But what *is* the status of curriculum model use among preschool teachers today — how many teachers consciously choose to use one model over another? To determine this, Epstein et al. (1996) conducted a survey of a random sample of early childhood practitioners who were NAEYC members. Of 2,000 questionnaires sent out, 671 (34%) were returned. The survey found that 33% of the respondents claimed to use a principal curriculum model — either High/Scope, Creative Curriculum, Kamii/DeVries, Montessori, Direct Instruction, Bank Street, or another specific model; 45% said they blended ideas from several curriculum models — making use of them but not committing to any one particular model; and 21% said they used no curriculum model at all.

This leads to the question of whether a teacher needs to be committed to a *principal* curriculum model. Certainly, commitment to a principal model would allow one to make the best use of research in the field. Research findings for curriculum effects can only be generalized to programs that use *essentially the same* curriculum models as those studied. If the program a teacher provides for children does not duplicate the elements responsible for a studied curriculum's effectiveness, then the research provides that teacher with no basis for expecting the same effectiveness from the provided program.

The challenge, however, in committing to a principal curriculum model lies in being able to distinguish essential from nonessential model elements. With respect to the High/Scope Curriculum, for example, it seems reasonable to conclude that the plan-do-review sequence is essential to program effectiveness, whereas snack time is not. Reciprocal teacher-child interaction is also very likely to be essential to the curriculum's success, but there may be a variety of ways that this interaction translates into elements of a daily routine. While painstaking research strategies might examine the various ways of being true to a single curriculum model, it is impractical to subject so many variations to the scrutiny of long-term research. Teachers are left, then, to strive for the long-term benefits identified by research by intelligently carrying out the curriculum model shown to produce these results. Note the use of the word "intelligently." Though commitment to a principal curriculum model is necessary to claim the effectiveness of that model, such commitment hardly requires the abandonment of any independent judgment, as some scholars have suggested (Goffin, 1993; Walsh, Smith, Alexander, & Ellwein, 1993). Situations in preschool programs are constantly changing; if teachers do not apply curriculum principles intelligently to these situations, their adherence to principles is reduced to mindless reactions.

How precise must one's commitment to a curriculum model be to claim its effectiveness? Model developers themselves convey a variety of opinions on this point. Some — such as Montessori and High/Scope — formalize (or even trademark) the names of their models and provide training and evaluation systems to maintain quality control of model implementation. Others do not formalize the names of their models: Russell Gersten writes about "direct instruction," not "Direct Instruction" (e.g., Gersten & Keating, 1987). DeVries prefers "constructivist education" to the "Kamii-DeVries" model (Epstein et al., 1996). This latter approach moves the curriculum model away from single individuals or institutions, obscuring the curriculum model's source of definition and possibly undermining the fidelity of implementation efforts. While more research is needed on how precisely curriculum models need to be defined and followed, *it is prudent to assume that a curriculum model of research-documented effectiveness must be followed closely but intelligently if similar effectiveness is to be achieved.* The results of the High/Scope Preschool Curriculum Comparison study suggest that preschool teachers should follow either the High/Scope model or the traditional Nursery School model.

To follow the High/Scope model, teachers can study the latest curriculum manual (Hohmann & Weikart, 1995) and other curriculum materials published by the High/Scope Press and they can participate in related training conducted by High/Scope consultants or certified High/Scope trainers.

Following the traditional Nursery School model used in this study presents preschool teachers with a greater challenge. They can study writings on the traditional Nursery School model (e.g., Sears & Dowley, 1963), or they can enroll in programs at the Bank Street College of Education or at a similar institution that espouses the traditional Nursery School curriculum. However, the Nursery School model used in this study had neither a specific, identified curriculum developer nor precisely defined rules of operation. Rather, it was meant to represent the accumulated wisdom and "good practice" of the early childhood field at that time.

But one cannot conclude from this study that it is enough to follow the accumulated wisdom of the early childhood field. Early childhood wisdom is as broad and diffuse as Direct Instruction is precise. While the curriculum comparison described in this book suggests that the accumulated wisdom is on the right track, our study hardly substantiates every idea that a good early childhood educator ever had. The Nursery School program in this study was a particular realization of time-honored early childhood curriculum principles, not the only possible realization of these principles. Because of this particularity, the program would be difficult to replicate.

This study may also be brought to bear on questions about the efficacy of parent involvement in preschool programs. Recall that biweekly 1½-hour home visits were part of the Direct Instruction program as well as of the High/Scope and Nursery School programs. Every effort was made to keep all aspects of these visits the same except insofar as they promoted different curriculum approaches. Therefore the findings reported here should dispel the belief that the *amount* of teacher-parent contact, by itself, makes the difference between a program that has lasting benefits and one that does not. But this study also suggests that the *content* of home-visits was an influencing factor. Study findings are consistent with the belief that substantial outreach to parents is a major vehicle by which a curriculum model exerts lasting benefits. Assuming that the home visits effectively communicated the various curriculum models to parents, Direct Instruction children experienced Direct Instruction not only in the classroom but also at home; High/Scope children experienced the High/Scope approach not only in the classroom but also at home; and Nursery School children experienced the Nursery School approach not only in the classroom but also at home. Thus, parent involvement could well have clinched the positive social effects of the two beneficial curriculums. Had the parents not been full partners in the implementation of the curriculum model with their children, perhaps the curriculum groups would not have differed significantly in their numbers of felony arrests.

The High/Scope Preschool Curriculum Comparison Study identifies the High/Scope Curriculum and a traditional Nursery School approach as particular methods of education that emphasize child initiative and thus develop in children the decision-making capacity and the social skills leading to greater success in adult life as responsible members of society. It indicates that these approaches, as opposed to a Direct Instruction approach, help children living in poverty avoid a later life of crime. It supports the claim that emphasis on child initiative, as realized in a defined curriculum model, is an essential part of the definition of good early childhood education.

References

American College Testing Program. (1976). *User's guide: Adult APL Survey.* Iowa City, IA: Author.

Andrews, D. A., Zinger, I., Hoge, R. D., Bonta, J., Gendreau, P., & Cullen, F. T. (1990). Does correctional treatment work? A clinically-relevant and psychologically-informed meta-analysis. *Criminology, 28,* 369–404.

Antonowicz, D. H., & Ross, R. R. (1994). Essential components of successful rehabilitation programs for offenders. *International Journal of Offender Therapy and Comparative Criminology, 38,* 97–104.

Arlin, M., & Hill, D. A. (1976). Arlin-Hill Survey. St. Louis, MO: Psychologists and Educators.

Arthur, G. (1952). *The Arthur Adaptation of the Leiter International Performance Scale.* Beverly Hills, CA: Psychological Service Center Press.

Bachman, J. G., & Johnston, J. (1978). *The Monitoring the Future questionnaire.* Ann Arbor, MI: University of Michigan, Institute for Social Research.

Barnett, W. S. (1996). *Lives in the balance: Age-27 benefit-cost anaylsis of the High/Scope Perry Preschool program* (Monographs of the High/Scope Educational Research Foundation, 11). Ypsilanti, MI: High/Scope Press.

Baumrind, D. (1971). Current patterns of parental authority. *Developmental Psychology Monographs, 1971, 4*(No. 4, Part 2)

Bereiter, C. (1986). Does Direct Instruction cause delinquency? *Early Childhood Research Quarterly, 1,* 289–292.

Bereiter, C., & Engelmann, S. (1966). *Teaching the disadvantaged child in the preschool.* Englewood Cliffs, NJ: Prentice-Hall.

Berrueta-Clement, J. R., Schweinhart, L. J., Barnett, W. S., Epstein, A. S., & Weikart, D. P. (1984). *Changed lives: The effects of the Perry Preschool Program on youths through age 19* (Monographs of the High/Scope Educational Research Foundation, 8). Ypsilanti, MI: High/Scope Press.

Bialer, I. (1961). Conceptualization of success and failure in mentally retarded and normal children. *Journal of Personality, 29,* 301–333.

Bissell, J. S. (1971). *Implementation of planned variation in Head Start.* Washington, DC: U.S. Department of Health, Education, and Welfare, Office of Child Development.

Bredekamp, S. (Ed.). (1987). *Developmentally appropriate practice in early childhood programs serving children from birth through age 8.* Washington, DC: National Association for the Education of Young Children.

Bronson, M. B. (1994). The usefulness of an observational measure of children's social and mastery behaviors in early childhood classrooms. *Early Childhood Research Quarterly, 9,* 19–43.

Burts, D. C., Hart, C. H., Charlesworth, R., Fleege, P. O., Mosley, J., & Thomasson, R. H. (1992). Observed activities and stress behaviors of children in developmentally appropriate and inappropriate kindergarten classrooms. *Early Childhood Research Quarterly, 7,* 297–318.

Burts, D. C., Hart, C. H., Charlesworth, R., & Kirk, L. (1990). A comparison of frequency of stress behaviors observed in kindergarten children in classrooms with developmentally appropriate versus developmentally inappropriate instructional practices. *Early Childhood Research Quarterly, 5,* 407–423.

Charlesworth, R., Hart, C. H., Burts, D. C., Thomasson, R. H., Mosley, J., & Fleege, P. O. (1993). Measuring the developmental appropriateness of kindergarten teachers' beliefs and practices. *Early Childhood Research Quarterly, 8,* 255–276.

Cohen, G. N., Bronson, M. B., & Casey, M. B. (1995). Planning as a factor in school achievement. *Journal of Applied Developmental Psychology, 16,* 405–428.

Datta, L., McHale, C., & Mitchell, S. (1976). *The effects of Head Start classroom experience on some aspects of child development: A summary report of national evaluations, 1966–1969.* (DHEW Publication No. OHD-76-30088). Washington, DC: U. S. Government Printing Office.

DeVries, R. (1991). The eye beholding the eye of the beholder: Reply to Gersten. *Early Childhood Research Quarterly, 6,* 539–548.

DeVries, R., Haney, J. P., & Zan, B. (1991). Sociomoral atmosphere in direct-instruction, eclectic, and constructivist kindergartens: A study of teachers' enacted interpersonal understanding. *Early Childhood Research Quarterly, 6,* 449–471.

DeVries, R., Reese-Learned, H., & Morgan, P. (1991). Sociomoral development in direct-instruction, eclectic, and constructivist kindergartens: A study of children's enacted interpersonal understanding. *Early Childhood Research Quarterly, 6,* 473–517.

Dunn, L. M. (1965). *Peabody Picture Vocabulary Test manual.* Minneapolis, MN: American Guidance Service.

Durost, W. N., Bixler, H. H., Wrightstone, J. W., Prescott, G. A., & Balow, I. H. (1971). *Metropolitan Achievement Test manual.* New York: Harcourt, Brace, Jovanovich.

Epstein, A. S. (1993). *Training for quality: Improving early childhood programs through systematic inservice training.* (Monographs of the High/Scope Educational Research Foundation, 9). Ypsilanti, MI: High/Scope Press.

Epstein, A. S., Schweinhart, L. J., & McAdoo, L. (1996). *Models of early childhood education.* Ypsilanti, MI: High/Scope Press.

Frede, E., & Barnett, W. S. (1992). Developmentally appropriate public school preschool: A study of implementation of the High/Scope Curriculum and its effects on disadvantaged children's skills at first grade. *Early Childhood Research Quarterly, 7,* 483–499.

Freeberg, N. E. (1976). Criterion measures for youth-work training programs: The development of relevant performance dimensions. *Journal of Applied Psychology, 61,* 537–545.

Gersten, R. (1986). Response to "Consequences of three preschool curriculum models through age 15." *Early Childhood Research Quarterly, 1,* 293–302.

Gersten, R., & Keating, T. (1987). Improving high school performance of "at-risk" students: A study of long-term benefits of direct instruction. *Educational Leadership, 44*(6), 28–31

Goffin, S. G. (1993). *Curriculum models and early childhood education: Appraising the relationship.* New York: Merrill.

Gray, S. W., Klaus, R. A., Miller, J. O., & Forrester, B. A. (1966). *Before first grade.* New York: Teachers College Press.

Hauser-Cram, P., Pierson, D. E., Walker, D. K., & Tivnan, T. (1991). *Early education in the public schools: Lessons from a comprehensive birth-to-kindergarten program.* San Francisco: Jossey-Bass.

Hindelang, M. J., Hirschi, T., & Weis, J. G. (1981). *Measuring delinquency.* Beverly Hills, CA: Sage.

Hirsh-Pasek, K., Hyson, M. C., & Rescorla, L. (1990). Academic environments in preschool: Do they pressure or challenge young children? *Early Education and Development, 1,* 401–423.

Hohmann, M., Banet, B., & Weikart, D. P. (1979). *Young children in action: A manual for preschool educators.* Ypsilanti, MI: High/Scope Press.

Hohmann, M., & Weikart, D. P. (1995). *Educating young children: Active learning practices for preschool and child care programs.* Ypsilanti, MI: High/Scope Press.

House, E. R., Glass, G. V., McLean, L. D., & Walker, D. F. (1978). No simple answer: Critique of the Follow Through evaluation. *Harvard Educational Review, 48,* 128–160.

Kagan, S. L., & Zigler, E. F. (Eds.) (1987). *Early schooling: The national debate.* New Haven, CT: Yale University Press.

Karnes, M. B., Schwedel, A. M., & Williams, M. B. (1983). A comparison of five approaches for educating young children from low-income homes. In Consortium for Longitudinal Studies, *As the twig is bent . . . lasting effects of preschool programs* (pp. 133–170). Hillsdale, NJ: Erlbaum.

Karnes, M. B., Teska, J. A., & Hodgins, A. S. (1970). The effects of four programs of classroom intervention on the intellectual and language development of four-year-old disadvantaged children. *American Journal of Orthopsychiatry, 40,* 58–76.

Karnes, M. B., Zehrbach, R. R., & Teska, J. A. (1972). The ameliorative approach in the development of curriculum. In R. K. Parker (Ed.), *Preschool in action: Exploring early childhood programs.* Boston: Allyn & Bacon.

Kennedy, M. M. (1978). Findings from the Follow Through Planned Variation study. *Educational Researcher, 7*(6) 3–11.

Kirk, S. A., McCarthy, J., & Kirk, W. D. (1968). *Examiner's manual: Illinois Test of Psycholinguistic Abilities* (Rev. ed.). Urbana, IL: University of Illinois Press.

Kohlberg, L., & Mayer, R. (1972). Development as the aim of education. *Harvard Educational Review, 42,* 449–496.

Larsen, J. M., Hite, S. J., Hart, C. H., & Robinson, C. H. (1994, November). *Do the positive effects of preschool persist through high school for students not at risk?* Paper presented at the annual conference of the National Association for the Education of Young Children, Atlanta, GA.

Larsen, J. M., & Robinson, C. C. (1989). Later effects of preschool on low-risk children. *Early Childhood Research Quarterly, 4,* 133–144.

Marcon, R. A. (1992). Differential effects of three preschool models on inner-city 4-year-olds. *Early Childhood Research Quarterly, 7,* 517–530.

Marcon, R. A. (1994, November). Doing the right thing for children: Linking research and policy reform in the District of Columbia public schools. *Young Children, 50*(1), 8–20.

McClelland, D., Hiatt, L., Mainwaring, S., & Weathers, T. (1970). *The Language Training Curriculum.* Ypsilanti, MI: High/Scope Educational Research Foundation.

McClelland, D., Martin, M., Malte, M., & Richardson, J. (1970). *The Unit-Based Curriculum.* Ypsilanti, MI: High/Scope Educational Research Foundation.

McClelland, D., Smith, S., Kluge, J., Hudson, A., & Taylor, C. (1970). *The Cognitive Curriculum.* Ypsilanti, MI: High/Scope Educational Research Foundation.

Medley, D. M., Schluck, C. G., & Ames, N. P. (1968). *Recording individual pupil experiences in the classroom: A manual for PROSE recorders.* Princeton, NJ: Educational Testing Service.

Meyer, L. A. (1984). Long-term academic effects of the direct instruction Project Follow Through. *Elementary School Journal, 84,* 380–394.

Miller, L. B., & Bizzell, R. P. (1983). The Louisville experiment: A comparison of four programs. In Consortium for Longitudinal Studies, *As the twig is bent . . . lasting effects of preschool programs* (pp. 171–199). Hillsdale, NJ: Erlbaum.

Miller, L. B., & Dyer, J. L. (1975). Four preschool programs: Their dimensions and effects. *Monographs of the Society for Research in Child Development, 40* (5–6, Serial No. 162).

Montessori, M. (1964). *The Montessori method.* New York: Schocken.

Norŭsis, M. J. (1993). *SPSS for Windows: Base system user's guide, Release 6.0.* Chicago: SPSS.

Pines, M. (1967, January). A pressure-cooker for two-year-old minds, *Harper's,* 55–61.

Rescorla, L., Hyson, M. C., & Hirsh-Pasek, K. (1991). *Academic instruction in early childhood: Challenge or pressure?* San Francisco: Jossey-Bass.

Reynolds, A. J. (1995). One year of preschool intervention or two: Does it matter? *Early Childhood Research Quarterly, 10,* 1–31.

Rosenberg, M. (1965). *Society and the adolescent self-image.* Princeton, NJ: Princeton University Press.

Sanders, G., & Haynes, D. (1985). *A preliminary study of students in Head Start, CAMPI Satellite preschools, and a comparison group* (Report No. 85-2). Seattle: Seattle Public Schools.

Schweinhart, L. J. (1994, January). Lasting benefits of preschool programs. *ERIC Digest,* EDO-PS-94-2.

Schweinhart, L. J., Barnes, H. V., & Weikart, D. P. (with Barnett, W. S., & Epstein, A. S.). (1993). *Significant benefits: The High/Scope Perry Preschool study through age 27* (Monographs of the High/Scope Educational Research Foundation, 10). Ypsilanti, MI: High/Scope Press.

Schweinhart, L. J., & Mazur, E. (1987). *Prekindergarten programs in urban schools* (High/Scope Early Childhood Policy Papers, 6). Ypsilanti, MI: High/Scope Press.

Schweinhart, L. J., & Wallgren, C. R. (1993). Effects of a Follow Through program on school achievement. *Journal of Research in Childhood Education, 8,* 43–56.

Schweinhart, L. J., & Weikart, D. P. (1980). *Young children grow up. The effects of the Perry Preschool program on youths through age 15* (Monographs of the High/Scope Educational Research Foundation, 7). Ypsilanti, MI: High/Scope Press.

Schweinhart, L. J., Weikart, D. P., & Larner, M. B. (1986a). Child-initiated activities in early childhood programs may help prevent delinquency. *Early Childhood Research Quarterly, 1,* 303–312.

Schweinhart, L. J., Weikart, D. P., & Larner, M. B. (1986b). Consequences of three preschool curriculum models through age 15. *Early Childhood Research Quarterly, 1,* 15–45.

Sears, P. S., & Dowley, E. M. (1963). Research on teaching in the nursery school. In N. L. Gage (Ed.), *Handbook of research on teaching.* Chicago: Rand McNally.

Smith, M. S. (1973). *Some short-term effects of Project Head Start: A preliminary report on the second year of planned variation, 1970–71.* Cambridge, MA: Huron Institute.

Stebbins, L. B., St. Pierre, R. G., Proper, E. C., Anderson, R. B., & Cerva, T. R. (1977). *Education as experimentation: A planned variation model, Volume IV-A, An evaluation of Follow Through.* Cambridge, MA: Abt Associates.

Stipek, D., Daniels, D., Galluzzo, D., & Milburn, S. (1992). Characterizing early childhood education programs for poor and middle-class children. *Early Childhood Research Quarterly, 7,* 1–19.

Terman, L. M., & Merrill, M. A. (1960). *Stanford-Binet Intelligence Scale, Form L-M: Manual for the third revision.* Boston, MA: Houghton Mifflin.

Tiegs, E. W., & Clark, W. W. (1963). *California Achievement Tests: Complete battery* (1957 ed.). Monterey Park, CA: California Test Bureau (McGraw-Hill).

U.S. Bureau of the Census. (1972). *Census of population and housing: 1970, Census tracts, Ann Arbor, Mich., Standard Metropolitan Statistical Area* (Final report PH[1]-11). Washington, DC: U.S. Government Printing Office.

Walsh, D. J., Smith, M. E., Alexander, M., & Ellwein, M. C. (1993). The curriculum as mysterious and constraining: Teachers' negotiations of the first year of a pilot programme for at-risk 4-year-olds. *Journal of Curriculum Studies, 25,* 317–332.

Wechsler, D. (1974). *Manual for the Wechsler Intelligence Scale for Children* (Rev. ed.). New York: Psychological Corporation.

Weikart, D. P. (1972). Relationship of curriculum, teaching, and learning in preschool education. In J. C. Stanley (Ed.), *Preschool programs for the disadvantaged* (pp. 22–66). Baltimore, MD: Johns Hopkins University Press.

Weikart, D. P. (1974). Curriculum for early childhood education. *Focus on Exceptional Children, 6,* 1–8.

Weikart, D. P., Deloria, D., Lawser, S., & Wiegerink, R. (1970, reprint 1993). *Longitudinal results of the Ypsilanti Perry Preschool Project* (Monographs of the High/Scope Educational Research Foundation, 1). Ypsilanti, MI: High/Scope Press.

Weikart, D. P., Epstein, A. S., Schweinhart, L. J., & Bond, J. T. (1978). *The Ypsilanti Preschool Curriculum Demonstration Project: Preschool years and longitudinal results* (Monographs of the High/Scope Educational Research Foundation, 4). Ypsilanti, MI: High/Scope Press.

Weikart, D. P., Rogers, L., Adcock, C., & McClelland, D. (1971). *The Cognitively Oriented Curriculum: A framework for preschool teachers.* Urbana, IL: University of Illinois.

Weisberg, H. I. (1973). *Short-term cognitive effects of Head Start programs: A report on the third year of Planned Variation — 1971–72.* Cambridge, MA: Huron Institute.

Zigler, E., & Muenchow, S. (1992). *Head Start: The inside story of America's most successful educational experiment.* New York: Basic Books.

The Quest for Delinquency Prevention With Lasting Effects

Rolf Loeber
Western Psychiatric Institute and Clinic, School of Medicine
University of Pittsburgh — Pittsburgh

The search for interventions to reduce delinquency has motivated many researchers and therapists but has rewarded few (Tremblay & Craig, 1995). Although some early interventions have reduced child-conduct problem behaviors, the results have not always been maintained (Wolf, Braukmann, & Ramp, 1987) or have not been in the desired direction, with the treated group becoming worse than the nontreated group (McCord, 1978). Thus, the quest for delinquency interventions with lasting positive effects has had a rocky history. The quest becomes even more ambitious when interventions take place as early as the preschool period, in an attempt to preempt delinquency several years before the children commit their first delinquent acts as juveniles, and several years before they become part of a subgroup of juveniles who continue to offend. Yet, this latter type of intervention would appear most meaningful, because for a proportion of persisting adult offenders, problem behavior dates back to their preschool years (Loeber & Dishion, 1983; Moffitt, 1993).

Lasting Differences concerns the outcomes of the High/Scope Preschool Curriculum Comparison Study and serves as a validation of the important findings from the High/Scope Perry Preschool Project (Berrueta-Clement, Schweinhart, Barnett, Epstein, & Weikart, 1984; Berrueta-Clement, Schweinhart, Barnett, & Weikart, 1987; Schweinhart, Barnes, & Weikart, 1993; Schweinhart & Weikart, 1980). The following comments concern misconduct and delinquency data in both studies and discuss the implications of the findings for the prevention of delinquency and for future experimental interventions. For that purpose, this commentary will contrast the High/Scope group in the comparison study with its two controls (the Nursery School group and the Direct Instruction group) and contrast the High/Scope group in the Perry study with its control (no-program group). This commentary will also address the various purposes of delinquency prevention, particularly whether the prevention applies to delinquents in general, repeat offenders, or chronic offenders.

Both the High/Scope Preschool Curriculum Comparison Study and the High/Scope Perry Preschool Project have major strengths: random assignment to experimental and control groups; follow-ups between ages 3 and 8; and subsequent follow-ups at age 10, at age 15, and into adulthood. Table C1 summarizes the results for delinquency measures of both studies. The average lifetime arrests were lowest in the High/Scope group in both the comparison study and the Perry study (but in the comparison study the

Table C1

DELINQUENCY OUTCOMES IN THE HIGH/SCOPE PRESCHOOL CURRICULUM COMPARISON AND HIGH/SCOPE PERRY PRESCHOOL STUDY GROUPS

Variable	High/Scope Group	Nursery School Group	Direct Instruction Group	No-program Group
Average lifetime arrests				
Comparison study	1.5	1.3	3.2[a]	—
Perry study	2.3	—	—	4.6
Adult arrests				
Comparison study	1.0	1.1	2.8	—
Perry study	1.8	—	—	4.0
Adult felony arrests				
Comparison study				
Age 17–21	.1	.3	.3[b]	—
Age 22–25	.1	.1	.6	—
Total adult	.2	.3	.9	—
Perry study (adult)	.7	—	—	1.5[b]
Juvenile arrests				
Comparison study	.5	.2	.3[b]	—
Perry study	.5	—	—	.6[b]
Juvenile self-reported misconduct/delinquency, age 15				
Comparison study	5.9	8.0	14.9	—
Perry study	5.2	—	—	7.1
Juvenile court petitions				
Perry study	.2	—	—	.4

Note. Table is based on data from *Lasting Differences* and Berrueta-Clement, Schweinhart, Barnett, Epstein, & Weikart,1984; Berrueta-Clement, Schweinhart, Barnett, & Weikart, 1987; Schweinhart, Barnes, & Epstein, 1993; Schweinhart & Weikart, 1980.

Results are statistically significant unless indicated otherwise; a dash means no value applies.

[a]Marginally statistically significant

[b]Not statistically significant

average for the High/Scope group was only marginally significantly different from that of the Direct Instruction group and was not significantly different from that of the Nursery School group). Nonetheless, the High/Scope group incurred half as many lifetime arrests as did the Direct Instruction group (means of 1.5 vs. 3.2). Also, the average number of adult arrests was lowest for the High/Scope group in both studies (but the High/Scope group in the comparison study was again nonsignificantly different from the Nursery School group). For example, in the comparison study the High/Scope group's average adult-arrest rate was about one third that of the Direct Instruction group (means 1.0 vs. 2.8).

In regard to serious forms of crime, the average number of felony arrests was significantly lowest for the High Scope group in the comparison study at age 22 and above (but this difference did not reach statistical significance at age 17 to 21), and the felony arrest difference was nonsignificant between the High/Scope and the no-program groups in the Perry study. Thus, overall, both studies provide substantial evidence of a reduction in lifetime and adult arrests. This evidence favors the High/Scope group in both studies (and the Nursery School group, as well, in the curriculum comparison study). However, serious forms of crime were lowest for the High/Scope group in the curriculum comparison study only at age 22 and above — not at age 17 to 21, which is often a peak period for offending (Farrington, 1986).

Arrest records reflect both police activity and participants' delinquent behavior. Convictions records, available in the Perry study only, show that the High/Scope group had a lower percentage of repeated undropped misdemeanor offenses than the no-program group, but the two groups did not differ on adult felony convictions (not shown in Table C1). Thus, the High/Scope program in the Perry study was associated with a reduction in police arrests and court processing of misdemeanor cases but not with a reduction in felony convictions.

Nevertheless, the important findings about the High/Scope program's ability to reduce delinquency in the adult years evoke the question of whether or not the program effects also apply to the juvenile years. Comparable intervention results for both adult and juvenile years are of importance in criminology, because the delinquency careers of some individuals start in late childhood or adolescence and are predictive of chronic offending later in life (Loeber, 1982). Both the High/Scope Preschool Curriculum Comparison Study and the High/Scope Perry Preschool Project included measures that address the issue of comparable results, because they included juvenile arrest records and self-reports, with the latter having the advantage of being a measure that is independent of police arrests.

Table C1 shows that the High/Scope group did not have a significantly lower juvenile arrest rate than the respective control group(s) in either the curriculum comparison study or the Perry study. The Perry study had available records of juvenile court petitions, which although they do not indicate that participants were guilty of delinquent acts, do indicate that there was substantial delinquency that warranted court processing. The total number of juvenile court petitions in the Perry study was half as large for the High/Scope group as for the no-program group. In addition, in the curriculum comparison study, the High/Scope group's average number of acts of self-reported misconduct/delinquency at age 15 was less than half that of the Direct Instruction group. Group differences on a similar measure in the Perry study, however, did not reach statistical significance. In summary, the results for juvenile delinquency are more mixed than the results for adult offending, but where significant delinquency differences were found, they favored the High/Scope group.

Overall, the findings should be seen in light of the fact that each study contained a relatively small number of participants — a fact that sets serious limits on the statistical power for detecting group differences. Limits to statistical power are even greater when applied to subgroups of participants, such as males compared with females, or African-Americans compared with Caucasians (the latter comparison being relevant only in the curriculum comparison study). Moreover, since delinquency records were available only for Michigan residents in the comparison study, the numbers in that study were even further reduced. (I understand that a request for FBI records, which would have covered participants' adult crimes committed anywhere across the country, was turned down by the FBI; Schweinhart, 1996.)

Since rates of delinquency and crime differ considerably by gender, it is important to ascertain whether the effects of interventions apply equally to males and females. The Perry study showed that the effects favored the High/Scope group over the no-program group, with the percentage of repeated lifetime arrests being lower for each gender when they had participated in the High/Scope program (not shown in Table C1). Results for repeated adult arrests were statistically significant for males but only approached significance for females. Even so, the fact that results applied to both genders is of considerable practical importance. Similarly, the curriculum comparison study reported significant curriculum group differences in felony arrests for both genders.

Researchers and practitioners in the field of criminology have become increasingly aware that a large proportion of juveniles offend at one time or another but that a smaller proportion commit serious delinquent acts, and an even smaller proportion become chronic offenders. Therefore, prevention programs can be evaluated in terms of how they reduce delinquency participation (also called prevalence), or re-offending, or chronic offending. Since chronic offenders are responsible for a disproportionate amount of the overall crime committed by juveniles (Farrington & West, 1993; Shannon, 1983; Tracy, Wolfgang, & Figlio, 1985; Wolfgang, Figlio & Sellin, 1972), the utility of a prevention program that addresses the chronic offender population is, of course, of highest importance.

In the High/Scope Perry Preschool study, mention was made of the High/Scope program's effect on repeat offending. A more detailed examination of available data shows that 2% and 5% of those in the High/Scope group were convicted for 3 to 5 or for 6 to 10 adult felonies, respectively; this compared with 8% and 5%, respectively, in the no-program group (overall chi-square significant). A similar analysis in the High/Scope Preschool Curriculum Comparison Study yielded nonsignificant differences. Given the small number of participants in both studies, these analyses probably had too little statistical power to properly address this question. Nevertheless, the results suggest that the High/Scope program can address very frequent offending.

Less resolved is the question of whether or not the High/Scope program addresses early onset, high-risk offenders (Loeber, 1982, 1988; Moffitt, 1993). These offenders typically have a first delinquent act prior to age 12 and are at risk for later continued, chronic offending (e.g., Loeber, 1982; Tolan, 1987). Given that the results for both the High/Scope Preschool Curriculum Comparison Study and the High/Scope Perry Preschool Project are mixed, it remains to be determined what impact the High/Scope program had on early-onset, high-risk juvenile offenders.

Despite this unresolved question, there is no doubt that the High/Scope program represents a pioneering effort to reduce later delinquency. The many similarities between the findings of the High/Scope Preschool Curriculum Comparison Study and the High/Scope Perry Preschool Project attest to the high preventive value of the High/Scope program.

References

Berrueta-Clement, J. R., Schweinhart, L. J., Barnett, W. S., Epstein, A. S., & Weikart, D. P. (1984). *Changed lives: The effects of the Perry Preschool program on youths through age 19* (Monographs of the High/Scope Educational Research Foundation, 8). Ypsilanti, MI: High/Scope Press.

Berrueta-Clement, J. R., Schweinhart, L. J., Barnett, W. S., & Weikart, D. P. (1987). The effects of early educational intervention on crime and delinquency in adolescence and early adulthood. In J. D. Burchard & S. N. Burchard (Eds.), *Prevention of delinquency* (pp. 220–240). Newbury Park: Sage.

Farrington, D. P. (1986). Age and crime. In M. Tonry & N. Morris (Eds.), *Crime and justice, Vol. 7* (pp. 29–90). Chicago: The University of Chicago Press.

Farrington, D. P., & West, D. J. (1993). Criminal, penal and life histories of chronic offenders: Risk and protective factors and early identification. *Criminal Behaviour and Mental Health, 3,* 492–523.

Loeber, R. (1982). The stability of antisocial and delinquent child behavior: A review. *Child Development, 53,* 1431–1446.

Loeber, R. (1988). Natural histories of conduct problems, delinquency, and associated substance use: Evidence for developmental progressions. In B. B. Lahey & A. E. Kazdin (Eds.), *Advances in clinical child psychology, Vol. 11* (pp. 73–124). New York: Plenum.

Loeber, R., & Dishion, T. J. (1983). Early predictors of male delinquency: A review. *Psychological Bulletin, 94,* 68—99.

McCord, J. (1978). A thirty year follow-up of treatment effect. *American Psychologist, 32,* 284—289.

Moffitt T. E. (1993). Adolescence-limited and life-cycle-persistent antisocial behavior: A developmental taxonomy. *Psychology Review, 100,* 674–701.

Schweinhart, L. J. (1996, May). Personal communication.

Schweinhart, L. J., Barnes, H. V., & Weikart, D. P. (with Barnett, W. S., & Epstein, A. S.). (1993). *Significant benefits: The High/Scope Perry Preschool study through age 27* (Monographs of the High/Scope Educational Research Foundation, 10). Ypsilanti, MI: High/Scope Press.

Schweinhart, L. J., & Weikart, D. P. (1980). *Young children grow up: The effects of the Perry Preschool program on youths through age 15* (Monographs of the High/Scope Educational Research Foundation, 7). Ypsilanti, MI: High/Scope Press.

Shannon, L. W. (1993). *Criminal career continuity. Its social context.* New York: Human Sciences Press.

Tolan, P. H. (1987). Implications of age of onset for delinquency. *Journal of Abnormal Child Psychology, 15,* 47–65.

Tracy, P. E., Wolfgang, M. E., & Figlio, R. M. (1985). *Delinquency in two birth cohorts* (Executive Summary). Washington, DC: United States Department of Justice, Office of Juvenile Justice and Delinquency Prevention.

Tremblay, R. E., & Craig, W. M. (1995). Developmental crime prevention. In R. E. Tremblay and W. M. Craig (Eds.), *Building a safer society, Strategic approaches to crime prevention* (pp. 151–236). Chicago, IL: The University of Chicago Press.

Wolf, M. M., Braukmann, C. J., & Ramp, K. A. (1987). Serious delinquent behavior may be part of a significantly handicapping condition: Cures and supportive environments. *Journal of Applied Behavior Analysis, 20,* 347–359.

Wolfgang, M. E., Figlio, R. M., & Sellin, T. (1972). *Delinquency in a birth cohort.* Chicago: The University of Chicago Press.

Lasting Differences: Can We Afford Not to Make Them?

George S. Morrison
Velma Schmidt Endowed Chair in Early Childhood Education
University of North Texas — Denton

Previous studies by Schweinhart and Weikart (1985, 1991, 1994) make it abundantly clear that investments in high-quality preschool programs produce over a sevenfold return for each dollar invested — through increases in high school graduations, reduced demands for social services, and reduced use of the justice system. These benefits are enough to justify the implementation of such programs. Additionally, data about the value of good preschool programs provide public-policy developers and legislators the information they need when making decisions about how to best allocate tax dollars and serve the needs of children, families, and future generations. Although program developers and legislators have not always wanted to spend now to save later, they nonetheless have the data to support such a policy.

Now, with the revelation that learner-centered pedagogy has other benefits as well, professionals have additional supporting data that make an even more convincing argument for high-quality preschool programs utilizing child-centered approaches. In *Lasting Differences,* authors Schweinhart and Weikart provide early childhood professionals and other policymakers additional information to think about: New data from their ongoing longitudinal study of preschool program effects argue against using Direct Instruction and for using a well-defined, constructivist curriculum model in preschool programs for young children. This recommendation is based on their finding that, compared with the Nursery School group and the High/Scope group, the Direct Instruction group had over three times as many felony arrests, especially felony arrests involving property crimes. This finding and its accompanying recommendation provide professionals with a welcome opportunity to discuss several important issues as they continually seek to determine how to best educate young children and teachers for the twenty-first century.

Perhaps one of the most serious and important questions Schweinhart and Weikart's data and recommendations raise is this: What program helps young children achieve greater success in life? When answering this question, Schweinhart and Weikart first strongly recommend that early childhood professionals should select the High/Scope approach as their curriculum of choice. Second, they remind us that the curriculum selection has great significance when viewed within the context that "Preschool teachers have an obligation not only to maintain children's immediate well-being but also to prepare children for the life that stretches before them" (p. 3).

Research results presented in *Lasting Differences* can help all early childhood professionals realize that the decisions they make do indeed transform and determine the life trajectories of children through adulthood. As Schweinhart and Weikart point out, there is much more to success than academic achievement. For some, this may mean thinking differently about the purposes of early childhood programs. What early childhood teachers believe about their practices and how they act on those beliefs both have a profound and lifelong influence on the behavior of their students. Teachers can no longer believe that their influence on children lasts only for an academic year and that they can pass children on to others with little or no consequence. Though it should come as no surprise that teacher practices have life-long influences, the results of the Schweinhart and Weikart study confront us again and again about the lasting differences professionals' decisions do make.

Implications for Educating Early Childhood Teachers

One criticism of the education of teachers is that it tends to promote authoritarian practices. Unfortunately, teachers perpetuate authoritarian practices for a number of reasons. First, many were taught that way in their youth. Second, in some teacher-preparation programs, teachers are not challenged to confront their own beliefs and practices, to change what they think, and to consider how beliefs affect practice. Third, some teachers are not educated in programs that promote constructivist practices supporting child-centered and child-initiated learning. Furthermore, some teacher-preparation programs encourage future teachers to have an eclectic approach. This is done in the belief that a smorgasbord of program ideas is superior to the basic tenets and practices of any one program model. In the name of eclecticism, educators of teachers contend that it is wrong to select and implement one particular program model. Even worse, as Schweinhart and Weikart point out in this monograph, some teachers believe it is best to use no program model at all.

At issue here is whether or not colleges of education and other teacher-training programs (such as alternative certification programs) should promote the use of program models that support child-centered learning to the exclusion of other approaches. The politics of such a decision are many and varied. First, teacher trainers are not unanimous in the belief that learner-centered curricula and programs are necessarily the best or only curricula. Second, some educators of early childhood teachers would make the argument that preservice preparation in any specific early childhood model is inappropriate, because teacher education programs should not give the impression of endorsing one model over another.

One way to encourage the use of constructivist approaches in early childhood programs, however, is through the use of a constructivist approach in teacher-training programs. When considering how to best prepare early childhood teachers for using a constructivist approach, we teacher educators have to make *learners* the focus of our endeavors. Traditionally teacher educators have emphasized the *process of teaching;* in this approach, teachers are the center of attention and are considered to be subject-matter experts who direct children's learning. However, in a learner-centered approach, the focus is on the learner rather than the teacher. States such as Texas have done a good job of prescribing learner-centered knowledge and skills as a basis for local programs and for teacher education (Texas Education Agency, 1996). However, there is no guarantee that such approaches are followed or implemented by education faculty. Restructuring colleges of education for learner-centered approaches is a vital prerequisite for making constructivist approaches a reality. "The politics of such an endeavor is interesting and demands that teacher educators change behavior patterns traditionally associated with teacher and student roles" (Condon, Clyde, Kyle, & Hovda, 1993, p. 277). Certainly many teacher educators have changed from a teacher-centered to a learner-centered approach, and others will continue to do so. However, in the absence of a planned and systematic effort, it is doubtful whether enough will opt to change so as to make lasting differences in the education of early childhood teachers. It may well be that in order to make lasting reforms in moving from teacher-centered to learner-centered approaches, the early childhood field will have to focus more on preservice education in Professional Development Schools and then use more inservice staff-development training, as the High/Scope program does. One of the greatest challenges facing trainers of early childhood teachers is to think and act in a constructivist way and to support and educate future teachers to do the same. Achieving this goal will require a great deal of unlearning. For, as Dona Kagan (1992) in her review of the professional growth of teachers points out,

> The personal beliefs and images that preservice candidates bring to programs of teacher education usually remain inflexible. Candidates tend to use the information provided in course work to confirm rather than to confront and correct their preexisting beliefs. Thus, a candidate's personal beliefs and images determine how much knowledge the candidate acquires from a preservice program and how it is interpreted. (p. 154)

Educating Parents

Early childhood professionals must work diligently to educate parents and the public about the content and results of best curriculum practices. The idea that authoritarian approaches work best is embedded in the beliefs of many parents and other stakeholders. A belief about the efficiency of authoritarian approaches leads some parents to embrace direct instruction and other forms of teacher-directed and content-centered education as "best practice." For many parents, academic achievement is all that counts in the education process. Unless they are provided with information to the contrary, parents, in the short term, may be little concerned with other areas of learning, such as initiative, social relations, and creative skills. Educating parents to this fuller dimension of schooling is a major challenge facing all involved in early childhood education. Also, there is much to be done in providing teachers and caregivers with the knowledge and training needed to help parents understand and embrace constructivist practices. If early childhood educators are to explain constructivist approaches to parents, they themselves will need to have a comprehensive understanding of the constructivist philosophy. Additionally, early childhood professionals must educate parents and the public about how to find appropriate early childhood programs for their children. If early childhood professionals hope to change practice, they also have to change parents' ideas about what constitutes good early childhood education.

Programmatic Decisions

Developing a learning-centered pedagogy should be one of the highest priorities for the nation's early childhood professionals. There are clear programmatic challenges for early childhood professionals as they consider learner-centered curriculum and pedagogy. One is at the program and classroom levels, where daily decisions are made about what to teach and how to teach it. On the one hand, the fact that curriculum selection helps to determine children's futures could lead to pessimism and helplessness. On the other hand, such a challenge will give well-meaning and dedicated teachers a renewed opportunity to pause and reflect on their practice. This reflection on practice is a process all early childhood professionals must engage in and promote as a way of changing and reforming practice. We should not let the results reported in *Lasting Differences* create the belief that the sky is falling; they should, however, make us think with greater clarity and responsibility about curriculum consequences for children.

Curriculum and Life Success

An important question is whether it is reasonable to attribute life success to the curriculum used in an early childhood program. Schweinhart and Weikart believe that to a significant extent it is, and they force us to think about this when they challenge early childhood professionals to confront the reality that they do touch and determine the future. However, to lay all the blame for life failures such as felony arrests at the feet of direct instruction is simplistic — the sources of criminal behavior are more complex than that. It is reasonable to also examine all of the variables within the broader contexts of family and community that can and do lead to wasted potential. If one of these factors is, as Schweinhart and Weikart suggest, the use of direct instruction, then professionals need to critically evaluate whether they should use such programs over others, while also considering how to change family and community conditions. For example, such out-of-school factors as home environment, community influences, and out-of-class time have influenced student learning nearly to the same degree as instruction (Wang, Haertel & Walberg, 1994).

The Direct Instruction Dilemma

Sometimes early childhood professionals engage in dualistic thinking, which supports the belief that one approach to the early childhood curriculum is better than another. Dualism isolates and compartmentalizes our thinking, leading us to take an either/or position. Abandoning a dualistic approach — in this case, an approach favoring either a child-centered or a direct instruction curriculum — would enable us to consider a more integrated approach. What would be helpful in such a process of integration would be a clear understanding of direct instruction. The Direct Instruction model reported in *Lasting Differences* was developed by Bereiter and Engelman (1966) and represents a rather programmed and rigid model, as found in the commercial program DISTAR. It is this model many think of when they think of a direct instruction model. However, a direct instruction approach that involves teachers making explicit what they want students to learn and actively teaching to achieve these goals is another form of direct instruction and one that has considerable support. According to Spiegel (1992),

> In direct instruction, students and teacher are focused on a goal or objective, on what is to be learned; students are aware of why it is important to learn the task at hand; and students are explicitly taught how to do a particular process through teacher modeling and explanation. (p. 41)

Additionally, approaches that utilize direct instruction methods can be quite effective with some children, particularly in the area of literacy development. Consequently there would appear to be value in trying to consider how the best of direct instruction and child-centered approaches can be used to help all children develop to their full potential. As Spiegel (1992) pointed out,

> I believe that bridges can and must be built between whole language and more traditional approaches to literacy instruction to enable teachers to blend the best of both in order to help every child reach his or her full literacy potential. Above all, we must avoid either/or positions that reject out of hand the possibility of blending and blind us to the value of different perspectives. (p. 43)

A fruitful area of discussion for early childhood professionals would be how to use the best of each approach to achieve common goals.

Achievement and Assessment Issues

Today there again seems to be a movement back to basic leading and learning. As this happens, assessment and power issues are at the center of decisions regarding curriculum and teaching methods. In such a climate, it may well be difficult to get some teachers and trainers of teachers to believe that teaching is not simply a matter of following the correct instructor's manual, one that is written by experts and designed to produce children who will score above average on a state or district achievement test. So, for many early childhood teachers who are pressured by parents and school districts, direct instruction becomes an attractive and alluring avenue to higher achievement-test scores. However, as the High/Scope Preschool Curriculum Comparison Study reminds us, short-term academic achievement cannot and should not be gained at the expense of undesirable lifetime behaviors.

Conclusion

At the heart of the question about which curriculum approach is best lie beliefs about what is worth knowing and how best to achieve this knowledge. This has to do with a moral dimension of teaching relating to core beliefs thought out and examined in the process of authentic teacher-education and other training programs. John Goodlad (1990), in commenting on the visits he and his colleagues made to colleges of education, commented on the absence of this moral dimension of teaching:

> The dismaying part of our learning during our visits to colleges and university campuses was the general failure of the institution to capture and build on the concept of teaching as a calling. Except in a few noteworthy instances, there was little or nothing in the recruitment literature and program descriptions to suggest the moral responsibility of the institution in taking on teacher education, the need to recruit people committed to dedicating their lives to teaching, an ongoing counseling effort to weed out the diffident, and a process during which those chosen were to be carefully socialized in their responsibilities as stewards of schools and mentors of the young. (p. 16)

Schweinhart and Weikart clearly remind professionals of their stewardship role as educators of young children. It is up to early childhood educators to make this vision a reality.

References

Bereiter, C., & Engelmann, S. (1966). *Teaching the disadvantaged child in the preschool.* Englewood Cliffs, NJ: Prentice-Hall.

Condon, M., Clyde, J., Kyle, D., & Hovda, R. (1993). A constructivist basis for teaching and teacher education: A framework for program development and research on graduates. *Journal of Teacher Education, 44,* 273–278.

Goodlad, J. I. (1990). *Teachers for our nation's schools.* San Francisco: Jossey-Bass Publishers.

Kagan, D. M. (1992). Professional growth among preservice and beginning teachers. *Review of Educational Research, 62*(2), 129–169.

Schweinhart, L., & Weikart, D. (1985). Evidence that good early childhood programs work. *Phi Delta Kappan, 66,* 545–551.

Schweinhart, L., & Weikart, D. (1991). Disadvantaged children and curriculum effects. *New Directions for Child Development, 53,* 57–64.

Schweinhart, L., & Weikart, D. (1994). *Lasting benefits of preschool programs* (Report No. EDO-PS-94-2). Urbana, IL: ERIC Clearinghouse on Elementary and Early Childhood Education. (ERIC Document Reproduction Service No. ED 365 478)

Spiegel, D. (1992). Blending whole language and systematic direct instruction. *The Reading Teacher, 46,* 38–44.

Texas Education Agency. (1996, September). *Texas Essential Knowledge and Skills.* Austin, TX: Author.

Wang, M. C., Haertel, G. D., & Walberg, H. J. (1994). What helps students learn? *Educational Leadership, 51,* 74–79.

The Quest for Quality in Curriculum

Kathy Sylva
Professor, Department of Child Development and Learning
Institute of Education, University of London

The monograph *Lasting Differences* describes research set in motion two decades ago to provide an answer to a question which is even more urgent today than it was then. Does preschool curriculum make a difference in the way young children develop into school learners, then adolescents, and finally adults in society? This report answers yes on the basis of a rigorous, longitudinal research design, but the yes is qualified here and there by scientific caution in the face of the study's small sample and its programmes of high intensity and investment. The study demonstrates that compared with a curriculum based on formal teaching, a "constructivist" curriculum centred on active learning leads to better outcomes for children.

This commentary has three aims:

- To consider *Lasting Differences* in the context of international policy debates
- To question the definition of *quality* assumed here and suggest one which has multiple dimensions
- To place the High/Scope Curriculum in a theoretical framework which owes as much to the work of Vygotsky as to that of Piaget

The Role of Research in the Global Expansion of Early Childhood Education

In 1992 Robert Myers wrote a powerful justification for worldwide early childhood education by summarising a massive body of research evidence demonstrating the beneficial impact on children, families, and communities of programmes implemented in centres, in homes, in work sites and under the shade of trees. The World Bank and UNICEF responded with new investment, and governments around the world have set aside funds for expansion of education and care before school (Sylva & Siraj Blatchford, 1996). European countries are no exception, with Spain, for example, mounting a large-scale national programme for children aged 0–6 years, under the auspices of the Ministry of Education.

There are two strands to the rationale for expansion in Europe: preschool education as a means of improving school performance, particularly for children from disadvantaged backgrounds (European Commission, 1995), and preschool services as a means of supporting families, especially those in which mothers seek employment or education (European Commission Network, 1996).

Expansion is uneven, of course, but in all countries there is fierce debate as to the kind of services, including curriculum, which should be sought. The newly formed European Early Childhood Education Research Association has convened several symposia to consider curricular issues across its member countries. Although sympathetic to a curriculum based on "developmentally appropriate practice" (Bredekamp, 1987), researchers and practitioners in Europe take the view that neither practices nor research findings can be transferred directly across cultures or national borders.

Must we then re-invent the wheel from town to town and country to country? No, there is a middle way which allows cautious generalisation of research findings across countries when two safeguards are met: The research study to be generalised must have strong internal validity, and it must be supported by similar research in the country or region to which the generalisation will be applied. The authors of this monograph are right to point to their many safeguards in the interest of internal validity: random assignment to condition, checks on programme implementation, robust and multiple outcome measures, tests or interviews carried out by persons "blind" to respondents' curriculum participation, and cautious statistical procedures.

The rigour of the research reported in this volume allows generalisation but cannot guarantee it. However, a well-designed study such as this, especially with random assignment of children to condition, is one important piece in a consistent pattern of research findings. It supports the view that in other settings, constructivist curricula such as the High/Scope model and the Nursery School model will have a positive impact, and Direct Instruction, a negative one. If other studies in other countries point in the same direction, we can be more confident in seeking constructivist approaches rather than formal, didactic ones.

Luckily there are evaluation studies in many European countries (see European Commission, 1995), and these too demonstrate that early childhood education can prepare children for successful schooling. Because there are few studies which make direct comparison between curricula and even fewer which employ random assignment to programme, it is important to debate the conditions under which well-designed studies such as the one in *Lasting Differences* can be generalised. Are there European studies which support the findings of the Ypsilanti study? One European study carried out in Lisbon, Portugal, by Nabuco and Sylva (1995) is outlined here because of striking similarities in method and results.

The effects of three preschool curricula in Portugal were measured via educational tests and social-emotional assessments at the start and end of first grade. The curricula included High/Scope, a Formal Skills curriculum, and a Traditional Nursery programme similar to the one in this monograph. They were deliberately chosen to represent three of the four curricular approaches in Figure 1 on page 25. Each curriculum was represented by five preschool centres, all chosen as "good examples of the model." When the children transferred at age 6 to primary school, control children with no experience of preschool were recruited from the same first-grade classes. In this design, children's academic and social progress over the first year in school was measured by comparisons with control children (classmates) who had not attended preschool, as well as with children who had attended nurseries implementing different preschool curricula.

The results of this short-term longitudinal study are in complete agreement with those of *Lasting Differences:* Children from the High/Scope nurseries showed significantly higher educational attainment (reading and writing), higher self-esteem (on the Harter Assessment of Perceived Competence and Acceptance), and lower anxiety than the matched control children. When compared with children in the Formal Skills group, the High/Scope children performed better on literacy tests, whereas children from the Formal Skills nurseries, when they arrived in first grade, were significantly more anxious and had lower self-esteem than the High/Scope children. When compared with the children in the Traditional Nursery, the High/Scope children showed better outcomes, although their superiority was comparatively less than it was in comparison with the Formal Skills group.

This study has been described as an attempt to establish a consistent pattern of findings across settings and countries. The results from Nabuco and Sylva's larger study (15 preschools, 3 curricula, 219 children) support the findings from the more rigorous but smaller study presented in this monograph. The findings from these two studies, as well as those of others not included here, tell a consistent story about the perils of preschool curriculum which is "too formal too soon." It takes a body of research and not one "magic bullet" study to provide a base to guide policymakers as they contemplate alternatives. Still more studies are required before a strong pattern emerges for each individual country.

A Multidimensional Definition of Quality

Lilian Katz (1995) was one of the first to list the many persons who could speak authoritatively on quality: children, parents, and teachers, as well as professional experts and researchers. In their conclusion to an edited volume on quality, Pence and Moss (1994) rejected what they call the *exclusionary* approach to defining quality in early childhood — the approach favoured as objective by scientific experts — and replace it with an *inclusionary* notion of quality. This new concept of quality is relative, values-based, and socially constructed by a host of different stakeholders.

The authors of *Lasting Differences* appear to assume that the curriculum which produces the "best results" will tell us which is of highest quality. Implicit in their work is the view that specification of "the quality curriculum" will be possible once lasting outcomes become known. In other words, they define *quality* as synonymous with the programme leading to the best results. The value basis of such quality judgments will become startlingly clear if we consider an imaginary curriculum which leads to high academic performance and reduced crime rates but which relies on corporal punishment or even the administration of tranquillising drugs to young children. Would we calmly claim the superiority of this "spank and drug" curriculum over all others on the basis of child outcomes alone? I doubt it, because sensible researchers and parents alike make judgments of *quality* on factors others than test scores or future home-ownership. Pence, Moss, and others are right to tell us that *quality* can never be an objective term.

There is a potential problem in the fact that acceptance of the inclusionary concept of quality may make it impossible to decide if one curriculum has more in its favour than another. Munton, Mooney, and Rowland (1995) summarise this problem, then suggest a resolution. If quality is relative, subjective, and defined by a chorus of stakeholders, they hint that it may prove impossible to make practical decisions at the national, state, or even local level. Stakeholders may disagree because they have different needs or because they see things from different angles. Because it is unlikely that the chorus of stakeholders will sing the same tune, Munton and his colleagues suggest that the search for one common definition of *quality* should be abandoned. In its place they call for a "universal framework within which definitions of quality can be deconstructed . . . a conceptual framework within which the values, beliefs and interests that underlie different definitions can be clearly explained" (p. 13).

Drawing on discussions about quality in medicine, Munton and his colleagues list the dimensions along which various definitions of *quality* may range; these include effectiveness, acceptability, efficiency, access, equity, and relevance. These authors argue that a deep understanding of quality depends on taking into account all the dimensions of quality. However any one study or policy exercise may choose to focus on just one or two of them. The authors of *Lasting Differences* do just this; they demonstrate very powerfully the quality dimension of effectiveness. If one seeks effectiveness at reducing crime, then the curriculum of highest quality will be one of a constructivist type, emphasising child initiative. It is this dimension of quality which concerns policymakers and a large number of parents (Henricson, 1994). However, we should be grateful to Katz, Munton, and others for reminding us that effectiveness is but one dimension of quality; others, such as acceptability or equity, are rarely the focus of outcome research, and they cry out for investigation too. To adopt an inclusionary definition of quality does not negate the power of outcome studies of effectiveness. It does however suggest that there may be other dimensions to consider as well.

Is High/Scope a Piagetian or a Vygotskian Curriculum?

The architects of the High/Scope Curriculum proudly proclaim their great debt to Piaget (Hohmann, Banet, & Weikart, 1979; Hohmann & Weikart, 1995) The curriculum's key experiences are the clearest example of the Piagetian influence (e.g., seriation, classification), but the whole High/Scope approach is couched in Piagetian terms. In this monograph, we are told about the theory behind High/Scope: "Based on Piaget's constructivist theory of child development, adults treat children as active learners and arrange their classrooms with discrete, well-equipped and labeled interest areas" (p. 26).

It has been argued (Sylva, 1992) that the theoretical basis of curriculum can be discovered in two ways: according to the theories which inspired the original developers, *but also* according to the theories whose principles are embodied within its aims, activities, interactional styles, and materials.

Despite the historical origins of High/Scope, its practice clearly embodies the Vygotskian principles of scaffolding, mediated learning, and cultural transmission (Sylva, 1992), and this needs to be acknowledged. The plan-do-review sequence owes little to Piaget but much to notions about experts who "scaffold" the learning of the novice. In small-group time, the adults who guide learning through their use of language are working within the "zone of proximal development" to extend children's thought. Those who develop and promote High/Scope may describe it in any way they wish (and their historical approach seems reasonable), but those who wish to understand the reasons for its impact may profit from other theorists who provide a reasoned account of cognitive development within culture. As a matter of fact, adding a Vygotskian slant to the High/Scope curriculum may lead to enhanced practices as the curriculum continues to evolve all over the world.

One of the most powerful parts of this monograph is the detailed, theoretical discussion of the ways in which Direct Instruction may "fail to prevent crime." Schweinhart and Weikart speculate on the importance of "feeling in charge of your life." They consider the "shared control" in High/Scope and Nursery School classrooms to be the moral environment of choice and negotiation. This insightful description of the mechanisms by which curriculum leads to good or poor social commitment in children is one of the most intriguing sections in the monograph. In it the authors present a new theory on deviance, one which takes into account the influence of the educational environment in shaping children's autonomy, decision-making, and feelings of control. These are the dispositions which appear to pull children away from deviant pathways.

Nabuco and Sylva (1995) found in their observations in Portugal that children in the Formal Skills nurseries had little choice over their activities, that Nursery School programmes allowed unlimited choice, and that High/Scope centres were somewhere in the middle; they enjoyed a balance of free and guided choice.

In the future, I expect there to be more detailed studies not only of the outcomes of different curricula but also of the microprocesses which bring about change in children's development. I have no doubt that the processes will be interactional ones and that Vygotsky's theories will illuminate the exciting ways that children acquire cultural tools, responsibility, and autonomy in early years classrooms.

References

Bredekamp, S. (Ed.). (1987). *Developmentally appropriate practice in early childhood programs serving children from birth through age 8.* Washington, DC: National Association for the Education of Young Children.

European Commission on Education, Training and Youth. (1995). *Pre-school education in the European Union.* Luxembourg: Author.

European Commission Network on Childcare and Other Measures to Reconcile Employment and Family Responsibilities. (1996). *A review of services for young children in the European Union 1990–1995.* Luxembourg: Author.

Henricson, C. (Ed.). (1994). *Crime and the family.* (Conference report from the proceedings of an international conference). London: Family Policy Studies Centre.

Hohmann, M., Banet, B., & Weikart, D. P. (1979). *Young children in action: A manual for preschool educators.* Ypsilanti, MI: High/Scope Press.

Hohmann, M., & Weikart, D. P. (1995). *Educating young children: Active learning practices for preschool and child care programs.* Ypsilanti, MI: High/Scope Press.

Katz, L. (1995). *Talks to teachers of young children.* Norwood, NJ: Ablex.

Munton, A. G., Mooney, A., & Rowland, L. (1995, September). Deconstructing quality: A conceptual framework for the new paradigm in day care provision for the under eights. *Early Child Development and Care, 114,* pp. 11–23.

Myers, R. (1992). *The twelve who survive.* London: Routledge.

Nabuco, M., & Sylva, K. (1995). *Comparisons between ECERS ratings of individual preschool centres and the results of target child observations: Do they match or do they differ?* Paper presented to the 5th European Conference on the Quality of Early Childhood Education, Paris.

Pence, A., & Moss, P. (1994). Towards an inclusionary approach in defining quality. In P. Moss and A. Pence (Eds.), *Valuing quality in early childhood services: New approaches to defining quality* (pp. 172–180). London: Paul Chapman Publishing, Ltd.

Sylva, K. (1992). Conversations in the nursery: How they contribute to aspirations and plans. *Language and Education, 6*(2–4), 141–148.

Sylva, K., & Siraj Blatchford, I. (1996). *The early learning experience of children 3–6: Strengthening primary education through bridging the gap between home and school.* Paris: United Nations Educational, Scientific, and Cultural Organization.

Using Knowledge in Communities: Personal Perspectives on Implications of the High/Scope Research

Valora Washington
W. K. Kellogg Foundation

Knowing is not enough;
We must apply!
Willing is not enough;
We must do.
— Goethe

The High/Scope Preschool Curriculum Comparison Study, along with the research of the High/Scope Perry Preschool Project, has had an enormous, positive effect on the field of early childhood education. Bredekamp (1996) articulates the gratitude that many early childhood professionals extend to High/Scope Foundation staff for their contributions to research, curriculum development, professional development, and advocacy. The High/Scope work, along with other notable longitudinal studies, has effectively transformed enthusiastic belief in the potential of early childhood programs into clear evidence of its lasting effects and cost-efficiency.

The current study, like other High/Scope work, is certain to become an instant landmark. Here Lawrence Schweinhart and David Weikart compare the relative effects of three curriculum models: High/Scope, Direct Instruction, and the traditional Nursery School. The researchers pointedly refute their own previous assertions that high-quality early childhood education could be built on any theoretically coherent model (Weikart, 1981). The Curriculum Comparison Study, first with age-15 data (Schweinhart, Weikart, & Larner, 1986), and then with evidence through age 23, distinguishes the programs in socially significant ways. The authors conclude that the use of Direct Instruction with young children living in poverty is "a risky path" that can lead to harmful effects. While the results of the study do not consistently distinguish between the long-term effectiveness of High/Scope and Nursery School, Schweinhart and Weikart conclude that it is a greater challenge to follow the Nursery School model because it lacks support materials and training like those offered by the High/Scope Educational Research Foundation.

This study has many implications for educational theory, research, and practice, as well as for public policy. If the past provides any insight into the future, our professional communities will review and debate these conclusions — both technically and conceptually — for many years to come. Drawing on my experiences over the past 6 years as a program officer for a private foundation, I would like to examine the implications of the study in the context of broader questions that the study brings to mind:

- As a profession, we know so much more about high-quality care and education for young children than is typically put into practice to benefit the overwhelming majority of our youngest citizens. How do we better use this knowledge to "bring to scale" best practices like those used in this study?
- At this time in our national history, there exists a strong movement toward devolution of responsibility and authority to state and local governments. How can our field effectively and strategically work through local communities?

Throughout its history, one of the foremost challenges of the W. K. Kellogg Foundation has been applying knowledge, particularly at the community level where life is lived, while working collaboratively and effectively with both the private for-profit sector and the public sector. With the experience of seven decades of the community-based approach, we recognize the challenges of knowledge utilization. Much of our work at the Kellogg Foundation is based on the assumption that in most areas of human endeavor, we in fact *know* better than we *do*. While we need to continually push the frontiers of knowledge, a greater challenge is to put into broader use what is already known.

Bringing to scale what are known to be effective developmental and educational strategies for young children is highly complex for many reasons. Within public education, which typically begins at age 5, it is considered to be the state's right to determine the appropriate curriculum and service-delivery mechanisms, so long as the state (or the particular locality to whom the right is entrusted) protects the constitutional rights of its citizens (lawful segregation by race, for example, is prohibited). Education for young children, however, is even more diffuse: Our nation has never decided to either create or endorse universally accessible programs for preschool children. Many programs operate in the private domain. And there has never been public or professional agreement that for most children, any specific curriculum is unquestionably superior to others. Rather, our field has been characterized by intense and not necessarily friendly competition among curriculum models.

Yet, within these restraints, important knowledge about appropriate education for young children has emerged. Over the past 30 years there has been tremendous expansion of research information about child development and early learning (Powell, 1995). Concurrently, practitioners, through their professional associations, have achieved consensus on principles of care as exemplified by a voluntary accreditation process (Bredekamp, 1987). The public has generally embraced this knowledge, as demonstrated by its willingness to invest in the federally funded Head Start program and a growing number of state-funded preschool initiatives targeted to low-income, at-risk children (Knitzer & Page, 1996).

The expansion of preschool programs has often, however, skirted both curriculum and quality issues. I have the impression that many citizens and even some educators incorrectly assume that Head Start represents a type of curriculum. In fact, the very useful and widely accepted "developmentally appropriate practices" (DAP) used by Head Start can lead to a *variety* of alternative curricula.

In my view, our professional challenge may be more fundamental than making an informed selection of High/Scope, Nursery School, Direct Instruction, or any one curricula over another. In my work, I have observed a few programs that did not appear to be based on coherent teaching strategies or an understanding of the vital role of curriculum. Other programs described themselves as using the DAP terminology but did not consistently apply its concepts. Supporting these observations, studies of early childhood programs indicate that approximately 10% of children of all income levels receive high-quality care, 60% receive adequate or custodial care, and 30% receive care that may be harmful (Powell, 1995). In reviewing the findings of the High/Scope Preschool Curriculum Comparison Study, few early childhood educators would debate the conclusion that the study "hardly substantiates every idea that a good early childhood educator ever had" (p. 70). Rather, the current study further points up disturbing ethical questions about why typical educational practices are not based on even the most well-documented knowledge of young children's needs.

The High/Scope Curriculum has been demonstrated to be a notable exception to the challenge of quality control. Critics have expressed doubts that the results of exemplary programs like the High/Scope Curriculum can be produced in typical or public school programs because of the need for higher salaries, better staffing ratios, and other factors (Powell, 1995; Frede & Barnett, 1992). Yet, the results obtained in these experiments are encouraging and show the paths toward specific outcomes. Because of these studies, we know what high-quality preschool education looks like — and that too few children actually receive it.

How then can and should we use the knowledge we have acquired, so the lessons learned about successful practices are more universally applied? In 1993, Weikart and Schweinhart noted that "delivery of high-quality programs is the most important task that the early childhood field faces, as programs move from laboratory and demonstration schools into large-scale service to children and their families" (p. 195). This curriculum study points to four clear challenges: (1) the need for leadership development and professional preparation within the field of early childhood care and education, (2) the challenge of promoting public understanding of quality care, (3) the value of effectively engaging community commitment to high-quality care, and (4) the importance of institutionalizing quality through legislative and administrative action.

Leadership Development and Professional Preparation

At the beginning of this decade a combination of leadership and professional preparation issues drew attention to a basic inadequacy of the early care and education systems. The majority of people who work with young children and their families were found to have little or no specialized training in the field of early childhood education. Given the weight of the evidence, it would be difficult to overstate the gravity of the impact of a poorly skilled, ill-compensated, discontinuous work force on the well-being and healthy development of children, especially infants and toddlers.

In response to the urgency of personnel issues, a variety of initiatives emerged. Professional preparation resources were buoyed by efforts of the Child Care and Development Block Grant, the Head Start Expansion and Quality Improvement Act, and the Military Caregiver Personnel Pay Plan. Now, however, the debate about quality seems largely stalemated as many of the recent modest gains stand to be crushed under the weight of escalating complexities such as devolution, diversity, and increased demands for services due to welfare reform and service integration (Phillips, 1994). These political and service-delivery complexities challenge even the most savvy and well-prepared professional — and certainly perplex a field that has not yet achieved solid institutionalization mechanisms to address human resources issues.

High/Scope is one of the few early childhood organizations that has been prepared over time to present a viable dissemination approach to a variety of practitioners on a large scale. There have been tests of the generalizability of the High/Scope Curriculum in large-scale, publicly supported programs both at the state level and in many school districts. It appears that programs implementing the curriculum at moderately acceptable levels were found to contribute to school success (Frede & Barnett, 1992; Bredekamp, 1996.)

Some of our colleagues have expressed cautions about large-scale application of the High/Scope approach. These cautions stem from several sources, including the animosity that has historically existed among various curricula, the appearance of self-dealing when an organization like High/Scope both researches and markets its products, and the "disempowerment" of teachers in the implementation process (Goffin, 1993; Walsh, Smith, Alexander, & Ellwein, 1993). Nevertheless, considering both the quality of the High/Scope work and the relatively few options, it is not surprising that these studies and the services offered fall on fertile ground.

Clearly, increasing broader community access to high-quality early childhood education programs will depend on a combination of efforts to create and sustain effective, broad-scale staff preparation. Delivery of professional preparation services will require a much larger investment of financial resources than currently exists. It is unlikely that the private sector generally, or foundations specifically, can provide resources on the scale needed. However, foundations can play vital facilitative roles in many ways. For example, they can reveal the specific supports or constraints that accompany knowledge transfer, especially in our culture of program diversity. Also, through their convening mechanisms, foundations might more directly advocate the importance of quality while leveraging increased private and public investments to the field. An encouraging prototype of this type of activity is a recent collaboration of at least 20 national foundations that are beginning to pool resources and expertise to create or sustain integrated systems of professional development for early childhood leaders. The collaboration aims to demonstrate how to expand, diversify, and mobilize the leadership capacity of the early care and education field in local communities, to develop the elements and visibility of a nationally recognized credential for directors of early childhood programs, to advocate the importance of quality in early care and education programs, and to help secure increased public and private investment in the field.

Promoting Public Understanding

The success of efforts to draw new or increased investments to the early childhood field depends on public will to act on information that illustrates the means for attaining tangible, measurable, quality improvements in the lives of children. In fact, without public will, remarkable research discoveries can lead to dissonance and frustration, as investments lag behind knowledge and opportunity. Now more than ever, promoting public understanding of the work we do must become a key strategy of our efforts to enhance program quality and to promote appropriate teaching strategies for young children.

Clearly, the onus is on the early childhood community to take the initiative to examine its role in the larger community and to stimulate public will. Professionals must continually seek opportunities to work in partnership with others and to "localize" their message. Consequently, we must expand issues of professional preparation to embrace such critical skills as political organizing, community mobilization, marketing, communications, team-building, and policy analysis (Families for Kids, 1995, 1996).

At the level of federal and state policies, previous High/Scope studies can be accurately credited with effectively disseminating the public message that "preschool works!" Yet media coverage may not have helped the reader to distinguish between an extraordinary experimental program and the more typical preschool resources that readers are likely to find in their own communities.

Scholars know, but the public may not be as keenly aware, that it is not enough to expand programs — we must also enhance child development. Additional effort is now needed to deepen public understanding around the more complex but essential components of what works: Specific teaching practices and children's experiences in the early childhood setting are important. This current study underscores this point, finding that specific types of preschool practices may not only be of limited value but may actually be harmful to the children who are typically eligible for publicly sponsored programs.

Receptivity to the "quality counts" message, or efforts to enhance quality, may be complicated for many reasons. Some publicly sponsored programs for young children may be created or expanded to facilitate another primary goal, such as enabling parents to move from welfare to work. Although a majority of states now offer preschool programs for disadvantaged children, research on their impact is quite limited (Knitzer & Page, 1996). In Michigan, for example, a state-funded part-day program was established in 1988 for 4-year-olds who show two or more critical "risk factors." Generally, the state has not played an active role in supporting curricula, staff preparation, or assessment of the overall effort. Obtaining and sustaining even minimal support for the evaluation or staff preparation needed to enhance effectiveness is a delicate challenge in the current fiscal and political climate.

Engaging Communities

As we enter this new century, success in expanding quality preschool services will depend to a great extent on our capacity to share this vision with others in local and community-inclusive contexts. These contexts include the ability to gather and analyze local information on program availability and quality as well as to engage communities in visioning and planning for young children.

For example, most successful child development programs, such as High/Scope, emphasize the critical role of working with parents. It stands to reason that to more broadly achieve these types of results, we must more actively engage parents (consumers) as advocates or spokespersons for children. Parent advocacy honors the rights and responsibilities of citizens in a democratic society to have some control over the policies and practices that affect their lives and the lives of their children. Parent and consumer knowledge can strengthen demand for well-defined, effective curricula, while the early childhood services themselves can empower parents (Washington & Oyemade, 1987).

Many foundations have been catalysts for mobilizing efforts for children and families that have evolved into statewide efforts (Knitzer & Page, 1996, p. 46). In a school-readiness initiative, the Kellogg Foundation worked with 20 local communities to provide support and technical assistance that would inspire localities to offer services to children in ways congruent with existing knowledge and local circumstances. It was apparent that local leaders highly valued the autonomy, discovery, and experimentation processes in their quest to enhance quality in their local communities; few expressed interest in "purchasing" resources such as High/Scope (Washington, Johnson, & McCracken, 1995).

Lessons from two Kellogg-Foundation-supported community visioning efforts led to important lessons about how to work through the processes of professional and community engagement. In one effort, a coalition of Michigan grantmakers sought to "jumpstart" change by offering child care training and technical assistance, promoting community planning, and providing a climate for open review of public policy (Larner, 1995; Sorenson & Washington, 1994). Another effort sought to promote a broad-scale reform in local and state child-adoption systems (Families for Kids, 1995, 1996). In both processes, community visioning proved to be an effective means of engaging the community commitment to the challenges of young children, of finding common ground on public issues of great importance, of using collaborative approaches to decision-making, and of honoring community power and diversity in decision-making. Several core elements of efforts to spearhead reform were identified: establishing a core leadership team, identifying stakeholders and obtaining their views, analyzing community input, developing consensus on reform directions, and maintaining community engagement throughout and after the initial visioning process. Establishing learning networks across states, so communities could learn from one another, was also important (Washington, Johnson, & McCracken, 1995).

A strong community voice, including community design of services, is essential. Apparently, professional preparation and community engagement processes require time to achieve if sustainable change is to occur. Training models that heavily depend on "days" of training are unlikely to be sufficient for some staff who are not already committed to and knowledgeable about DAP; frequent on-site support may also be another useful feature of professional preparation or community engagement. Yet, nowhere is this investment of time, skill, and experience more valuable than it is in programming that affects the lives of children and families, particularly those who are isolated and vulnerable.

Strengthening Legislative Relationships

Community visioning ultimately spotlights the need for systemic legislative or administrative reform, an area of work in which High/Scope staff have a good deal of experience. In the case of early childhood services generally, however, it quickly becomes apparent that the field has weak relationships with legislative bodies. If we intend to bring programs to scale using increased public resources, these relationships must be fortified.

A recent study of state legislative leaders is illustrative. Only a few of these leaders expressed familiarity with widely disseminated research relating to children and families. Some have seen reports concerning children but have not read them and were unable to provide any detail concerning their content. Moreover, early childhood advocates were "invisible" to these legislators; when visible, they were viewed as lacking a coordinated, manageable legislative agenda and well-defined goals. The leaders felt that at times, these groups seemed to be competing with one another. Yet clearly, it is within these 7,500 state legislative districts that strategic action can and must be mobilized if high-quality care and education is ever to move to scale (State Legislative Leaders Foundation, 1995).

Relationships with legislative leaders are particularly important, because many of the components of quality (such as group size; staffing ratios; program standards; and staff qualifications, certification, or preparation requirements) are within the scope of state regulatory standards. As advocates work to bring programs to scale, we must recognize that state regulations have near-universal impact as well as demonstrated effectiveness in improving quality. Any effort to bring programs to scale must include raising these standards through legislative and administrative advocacy, as well as drawing attention to the complex funding-subsidy programs that also influence the quality of care through state-level directives.

State regulations are not a panacea, however. They vary from state to state, are often inconsistent across funding streams, and occur within different historical contexts (Morgan et al., 1993; Besharov, 1996). One cannot assume that state regulations are sufficient to ensure adequate implementation of DAP; substantial resources also must be devoted to a system of evaluating actual classroom practices and training (Frede & Barnett, 1992).

Foundations could play a more active role in facilitating relationships and outreach with state legislative and administrative leaders — and also with the leaders on whom these legislators rely for information (media, business, and civic leaders). Foundations could also help nonprofit organizations to clarify and better understand what they can and cannot do within the boundaries of their nonprofit status to help these legislative bodies become more informed and engaged on behalf of children's issues (State Legislative Leaders Foundation, 1995).

Summary

The human condition can be improved by the appropriate use of knowledge, science, and technology. Significant progress has been made in establishing both a solid research foundation and principles of practice that could enhance our capacity to nurture and invest in children. The good news is that states have responded well to this knowledge by creating and sustaining new programs for early childhood services. However, quality and curriculum issues are sometimes neglected in this process. As a wide array of programs of varying quality have emerged to serve young children, the capacity to select curriculum has been complicated by a host of more fundamental challenges. The resulting chasm between knowledge and practice presents significant ethical and policy challenges that are likely to be magnified in the current climate of both fiscal austerity and government devolution of authority.

Specifically, the many implications of the High/Scope Preschool Curriculum Comparison Study include concern about how our nation might best bring to scale the teaching strategies and experiences that have proved to be effective with young children. I have suggested an integration of strategies that include leadership development within the field, public education, public engagement, and legislative/administrative action.

Organizations such as High/Scope have demonstrated the research strength and institutional capacity to effectively transfer knowledge on a larger scale. Their capacity includes a high-quality curriculum, training and support materials, and tools to assess implementation. While there are criticisms of this approach, critics offer woefully few alternatives for how we might draw upon the lessons of significant long-term research and apply them to practice. Obviously, children are not well-served in an atmosphere of public or professional inertia.

There is an urgent need for the early childhood professional community — and local and state providers of services — to more fully consider ways to transfer and institutionalize best practices, so every child can be assured of a high-quality preschool education. The solutions do not by any means lie in a top-down imposition of curricula; they do lie in a fuller understanding of the concepts and principles underlying curricula, and to achieve this understanding requires both professional and community time — time to vision, learn, and plan together.

Foundations can assist in this effort by identifying and focusing on those areas where private funding is most likely to make a difference — areas that receive inadequate funding or that leverage public- and private-sector support through advocacy, community-based processes, or the modeling of innovative programs. In this way, our nation can move beyond mere rhetoric about "the value of prevention over treatment" and toward achievement of the long-lasting social benefits of early childhood education.

References and Resources

Behrman, R. E. (Ed). (1995). *The future of children: Long-term outcomes of early childhood programs.* Los Altos, CA: The Center for the Future of Children, The David and Lucile Packard Foundation.

Besharov, D. J. (Ed). (1996). *Enhancing early childhood programs: Burdens and opportunities.* Washington, DC: Child Welfare League of America and American Enterprise Institute for Public Policy Research.

Bredekamp S. (Ed). (1987). *Developmentally appropriate practice in early childhood programs serving children from birth to age 8* (Exp. Ed.). Washington, DC: National Association for the Education of Young Children.

Bredekamp, S. (1996). 25 years of educating young children: The High/Scope approach to preschool education. *Young Children, 51*(4), 57–61.

Erwin, E. (Ed). (1996). *Putting children first: Visions for a brighter future for young children and their families* (pp. 55–75). Baltimore, MD: Paul H. Brookes Publishing Co.

Families for kids: Building the dream. (1995). Battle Creek, MI: W. K. Kellogg Foundation.

Families for kids who wait: Promising directions in community-based adoption reform. (1996). Battle Creek, MI: W. K. Kellogg Foundation.

Frede, E., & Barnett, W. S. (1992). Developmentally appropriate public school preschool: A study of implementation of the High/Scope Curriculum and its effects on disadvantaged children's skills at first grade. *Early Childhood Research Quarterly, 7,* 483–495.

Galinsky, E., & Friedman, D. (1993). *Education before school: Investing in quality child care.* New York: Scholastic.

Goffin, S. G. (1993). *Curriculum models and early childhood education: Appraising the relationship.* New York: Macmillan College Publishing Co.

Knitzer, J., & Page, S. (1996). *Map and track: State initiatives for young children and families.* New York: National Center for Children in Poverty.

Larner, M. (1995). *Jumpstarting change: A report on joining forces, The Michigan Grantmakers Conference on Child Care.* Unpublished report, W. K. Kellogg Foundation.

Morgan, G., Azer, S., Costley, J., Genser, A., Goodman, I., Lombardi, J., & McGimsey, B. (1993). *Making a career of it: The State of the States Report on career development in early care and education.* Boston, MA: Wheelock College.

Philips, D. A. (1994). *Reconsidering quality in early care and education* (Quality 2000 Working Paper). Washington, DC: National Research Council/Institute of Medicine.

Powell, D. R. (1995). *Enabling young children to succeed in school.* Washington, DC: American Education Research Quarterly.

Schweinhart, L. J., Weikart, D. P., & Larner, M. B. (1986). Consequences of three preschool curriculum models through age 15. *Early Childhood Research Quarterly, 1,* 15–45.

Sorenson, P., & Washington, V. (1994). *Joining forces: Strengthening the circle of caring communities for children.* Battle Creek, MI: W. K. Kellogg Foundation.

State Legislative Leaders Foundation. (1995). *State legislative leaders: Keys to effective legislation for children and families.* Centerville, MA: Author.

Walsh, D. J., Smith, M. E., Alexander, M., & Ellwein, M. C. (1993). The curriculum as mysterious and constraining: Teachers' negotiations of the first year of a pilot programme for at-risk four-year-olds. *Curriculum Studies, 25*(4), 317–332.

Washington, V., Johnson, V., & McCracken, J. (1995). *Grassroots success! Preparing schools and families for each other.* Battle Creek, MI: W. K. Kellogg Foundation.

Washington, V., & Oyemade, J. (1987). *Project Head Start: Past, present, and future trends in the context of family needs.* New York: Garland.

Weikart, D. P. (1981). Effects of different curricula in early childhood intervention. *Educational Evaluation and Policy Analysis, 3,* 25–35.

Weikart, D. P., & Schweinhart, L. (1993). The High/Scope Curriculum for early childhood care and education. In J. L. Roopnarine and J. E. Johnson (Eds.), *Approaches to early childhood education* (2nd Ed., pp. 195–208). New York: Merrill/Macmillan.

Zigler, E. F., Kagan, S. L., & Klugman (Eds). (1983). *Children, families and government: Perspectives on American social policy.* Cambridge: Cambridge University Press.

Index